THE SCHOOL DAY
BEGINS

THE SCHOOL DAY BEGINS

A GUIDE TO OPENING EXERCISES

Grades Kindergarten—12

COMPILED BY

AGNES KRARUP AND ASSOCIATES

Pittsburgh Public Schools

Third Edition

HOBBS, DORMAN & COMPANY, INC.

New York Buenos Aires

Library of Congress Card Number: 67-23660

Printed in the United States of America

FOREWORD

When our schools opened in September 1963, following the Supreme Court's ruling that prayer and Bible reading in school were incompatible with the Constitution, we agreed as a faculty to seek other means of fostering values in our schools. Recalling our *Newsletter* of October 1963:

> "When all is said and done, the opening exercises, before and after the Supreme Court decision, are concerned with *values*. These values now take on a potential of broader and deeper dimensions. We can teach the brotherhood of man without actual use of the Scripture; we can teach integrity without ritual; we can teach the ethic of love without prayer. And there remain many other values woven through our narrative literature, our poetry, our biographies, our music, our art that present a vast opportunity for the constructive uses of these precious five minutes a day. These five minutes become something over 250 hours in the years the child is with us."

To give support and consistency to the proposition that we can preserve and possibly increase the worth of the morning exercises, I asked a committee of staff members under the chairmanship of Miss Agnes Krarup to study this subject. They were asked to develop a guide for the use of all teachers and principals in the continued fruitful conduct of morning exercises in the Pittsburgh schools. They grouped themselves into four levels: kindergarten-primary, intermediate, junior high, and high school. They have gathered materials from throughout our schools, and added creative contributions of their own. The committee included teachers, principals, librarians, and supervisors at all levels. The product is this collection of ideas and promising practices.

A first draft of this publication was produced in the fall of 1964, and was field tested during the early half of the school year. Many constructive additions and revisions were contributed by teachers throughout the system in achieving this finished edition.

I extend to Miss Krarup and her committee and to all who contributed materials the warm thanks of the faculty for the excellence of their work.

SIDNEY P. MARLAND, JR.
Superintendent of Schools
Pittsburgh, Pennsylvania

THE EDITORIAL COMMITTEE

AGNES KRARUP — *Chairman*
Director of School Library Services

EVAN W. INGRAM — *Consultant*
Assistant Superintendent for Curriculum
and Instruction (Ret.)

MARY L. MOLYNEAUX — *Consultant*
Assistant Superintendent for Curriculum
and Instruction

Subcommittee/Grades K–3

FLORENCE LEARZAF — *Chairman*
Principal/John Morrow School

LIVIETTE LANGER — Primary teacher/Linden
MARION D. BENJAMIN — Art teacher/Linden
ANNA W. HARKINS — Supervisor/School Library Services
GRACE WOOD — Primary Supervisor
BERTHA BAILEY — Library Supervisor

Subcommittee/Grades 4–6

ROBERT DOERSCHNER — *Chairman*
Principal/Baxter School

WILLA WHITE — Supervisor/General Elementary Education
ANGELA CRAWFORD — Music teacher/Liberty
BETTY HEARD — Librarian/Manchester (Resigned)
NANCY LUTZ — Supervisor/General Elementary Education
BERTHA BAILEY — Library Supervisor

Subcommittee/Grades 7–9

FRANCIS RIFUGIATO — *Chairman*
Director of Curriculum

RUTH RICHEY — English team leader/Herron Hill (Ret.)
MARIE STEWART — Social Studies teacher/Mifflin
CLARE BUCKLEY — Librarian/Latimer
LOIS M. GROSE — Associate Director of Instruction for English
AGNES KRARUP — Director/School Library Services

Subcommittee/Grades 10–12

CARL BRACKMAN — *Chairman*
Principal/Carrick Senior High School

STELLA PRICE — Head of English Department/South Hills (Ret.)
EULALIA SCHRAMM — Head of Social Studies Department/Peabody (Ret.)
GERTRUDE OETTING — Librarian/Allderdice (Resigned)
PAUL DREIBELBIS — Associate Director of Instruction for Social Studies
AGNES KRARUP — Director/School Library Services

CONTENTS

FROM COURTROOM TO CLASSROOM

On June 17, 1963, the Supreme Court of the United States ruled it unconstitutional that public schools require at the beginning of each school day readings from the Holy Bible or the recitation of the Lord's Prayer in solo or in unison.

On August 23, 1963, Walter E. Alessandroni, attorney general, and John D. Killian III, deputy attorney general of Pennsylvania, issued a concurring opinion, declaring that:

> "Group Bible reading and prayer . . . as the practices have heretofore existed as devotional exercises or ritual in the public schools, cannot continue in the public schools, whether or not they are required or permitted by school boards, administrators, or teachers, and whether or not the pupils engage in the practices voluntarily, or even with the express written consent of their parents."

Admittedly, it is hard for us in the Pittsburgh Public Schools—as it is elsewhere throughout America—to drop the practice of beginning the school day with a religious ritual. It is hard also to resist concluding a minute of silent meditation with the word "amen." It is hard not to include hymns in the group singing as part of the opening exercises; but the ruling of the Supreme Court is now the law of the land and school practices must be in accord with it. What then remains? The Pennsylvania attorney general goes on to say:

> ". . . The following nonreligious practices may be substituted lawfully in the public schools in place of corporate prayer and Bible reading without offending the First Amendment: daily recitation of the Pledge of Allegiance; a period of silent meditation; readings from great literature, messages and speeches of great Americans and from other documents of our heritage; presentation of inspirational music, poetry, and art."

The materials in this manual have been selected so that schools and teachers can plan opening exercises acceptable under the law yet inspirational and appropriate for beginning the day. Since September 1963, our schools have been trying new practices, using nonreligious materials. Much of what they have developed is included here.

May these quotations and others like them from the wise men of ancient times or modern, these bits of verse, these apostrophes to country, give our pupils insight into greatness, into courage, into loyalty, devotion and other high qualities that their lives may be enriched, not just for the moment, but for all their growing years and throughout life.

EVAN W. INGRAM
Associate Superintendent
for Instruction (Ret.)
Pittsburgh Public Schools

INTRODUCTION

PRINCIPLES AND CRITERIA FOR OPENING EXERCISES

A day in school should always begin with an affirmative tone. Children and young people should have their spirits lifted; they should enjoy together a sense of security, of unity of purpose, and of hope for the day's work. This guide to opening exercises is intended to suggest some activities and some criteria that will help achieve a good beginning for the school day. It does not intend the establishment of a uniform pattern for all. We hope rather that it will spark creative thinking and at the same time serve as an immediate resource.

Subcommittees for four grade groups [kindergarten-3, 4-6, 7-9, and 10-12] have formulated several acceptable patterns, with activities and representative materials appropriate to the pupils at each grade level. As they have worked, they have used the specific and practical plans developed and sent in by faculty committees. Principals and faculty or student committees will in turn wish to make their own adaptations of this manual to the needs of their schools. *It should be remembered that this is a source book and not simply a how-to-do-it manual.*

As the subcommittees sorted and arranged suggestions submitted by the multiplicity of contributors, and as they began to clarify their own thinking, certain underlying ideas and criteria began to emerge.

Amount of Time

When the Supreme Court ruled out the Lord's Prayer and Bible reading, the time released from the usual ten-minute schedule of opening exercises was approximately three minutes. Teachers and principals may choose to make the new exercises somewhat longer than this, but the time actually available is too limited for certain activities to be practical, unless they can be carried on over a period of days.

The committee has been chiefly concerned, then, in determining what it is that schools can do in a period of three to seven minutes. Whatever is done should be worthy of this significant portion of the day, yet suitable for the widely varying levels of maturity from kindergarten through the twelfth grade. Material presented should raise standards of student appreciation, not merely echo present standards.

Format and Subject Matter

The committee thinks that a daily or weekly format is desirable. Children will feel a sense of order in the day's beginning as they become familiar with the underlying pattern. Schools will want to plan, however, so that within the pattern there will be room for variations [different poems or songs or readings], and even complete departures for special occasions. The list of themes, the list of days and weeks to be celebrated, and the other resources in the guide are intended to suggest variety of this kind.

It is not necessary to find a constantly changing selection of poems, prose, and songs. Some teachers may prefer to achieve a sense of continuity by reading the same prose excerpt or poem every day for a week or longer, permitting children to join in as they become familiar with phrases or verses.

The presentation should always be keyed to the level of student understanding, with sufficient explanation to make its content meaningful to the listeners.

Teacher Attitude

The attitude of the teacher toward the opening exercises period is extremely important. The manner of presentation will determine its effectiveness as much as the choice of themes and activities. Words may be forgotten, but the value the teacher places on truth, goodness, and beauty will long be remembered. These values, like other spiritual qualities, are frequently "caught" rather than taught. Hence the tone set by the teacher will not only affect the immediate response of the children; but it will, in many instances, influence their subsequent behavior as well. The teacher will, therefore, strive toward a feeling of some formality, seriousness, dignity, and inspiration.

Public Address or Class Observance

In some schools a good public-address system offers an opportunity for all students to participate in opening exercises together. Music can be broadcast, if the tone of the public-address system permits, but provision should be made for extremes of the children's growth and development. Preparing a single program suitable for both kindergarten and eighth grade or for grades 7-12 is not easy. For this reason many teachers prefer to conduct their own opening exercises adapted to their pupils' interests and abilities. Such a teacher-led program is usually more effective than one presented over the public-address system.

Use of Students

Although, generally speaking, faculty committees will plan the opening exercises, schools may appoint student committees to help search for materials. Students can be especially helpful in preparing, under teacher guidance, brief paragraphs concerning the significance of the days or weeks that have been listed in connection with this guide. Some schools will prepare students to read over the public-address system. They must be carefully trained so that they do not inflict an inexpert performance upon the school as a whole. Other schools will use student musical or choral speaking groups. Here, as in every aspect of our opening exercises, standards must be high.

Sources of Materials

Seasonal poems of real beauty may awaken in a child or an adolescent a sense of wonder about the universe. These can be found in the many excellent anthologies of poetry for children and young people in our school libraries. Many pleasant little verses relating to the seasons or to the holidays fall short of real merit for opening exercises although they may be relevant to classroom lessons.

Newspapers are excellent sources for quotations from current speeches, proclamations, and quotations from great men.

In the elementary schools, children sometimes voluntarily bring meaningful paragraphs from their reading to the attention of their teachers. Since there are many thoughtful and inspirational passages in well-written children's books, this activity can be valuable, provided that children understand that all contributions must measure up to a high standard.

Teachers of creative writing may occasionally find something of such subtle sensitivity and beauty coming from a highly gifted child that its suitability for opening exercises is immediately apparent. This occurrence is admittedly rare; nevertheless, it offers a student resource that should not be overlooked.

Music

Beautiful music for quiet listening or patriotic songs and marches on days that call for them should be included for all grades. Only music which is well written and excellently performed should be used. In the elementary schools, group singing within the classroom is excellent for opening exercises.

Religious Holy Days and Holidays

The holy days and holidays of the major religious faiths can be acknowledged in a way that will help children respect differences and appreciate freedom of religion. Any expression of preference for one religion over another or any element of religious ritual must be avoided.

Explanations of the major religious holy days and holidays have been respectfully presented in several books. The objective approach in these will serve as a guide and the information as a resource.

Silent Reflection

Almost universally our schools are using one full minute of silent reflection, a practice that has apparently won quick acceptance among the children. To give *one full minute* is important because it is all too brief a time for children to gather their thoughts on what they hope to do that day, contemplate the thought for the day, or say a silent prayer, if they wish. Children will soon grow accustomed to the full minute. In some schools the silence is broken by a repetition of the thought for the day or by repetition of the last verse of the poem read previously. Elementary school teachers often break it with group singing. In any case the completed period of opening exercises should be followed by a brief pause to mark it off from the roll call or the daily bulletin.

Standards for Presentation

From kindergarten on, ideas should be introduced that will help children to live their lives effectively for themselves, for others, and for their country. High ideals and the beginnings of a philosophy should result from this program.

The time may be ripe for our students to absorb their vital heritage by hearing again and again imperishable words from our country's past. Enough paraphrasing and explanations should be given so that children understand such things as the Pledge of Allegiance, the Declaration of Independence, the Preamble to the Constitution, or the Bill of Rights.

When the magic of a selection lies in the beauty of its wording, however, discussions as to its meaning should be held to a minimum. If children do not at first fully comprehend all of what is being read, they are nevertheless capable of some appreciation if the selection has enough intrinsic merit. Comprehension of the superficial is easy; comprehension of the significant is more difficult and comes only with thought and familiarity.

This committee thinks that the principal of each school is responsible for setting the general tone of opening exercises in his building. He may, however, delegate much of the planning to committees. The four sections that follow are arranged according to grade levels. Each gives several suggested patterns for opening exercises with activities, themes, and selections. As would be expected, a subtle change in tone and approach is perceptible as one moves through the elementary grades into the secondary school. Yet any committee will find it profitable to read every section for ideas that can be adapted. It is our hope that the suggestions given here will assist committees, teachers, and principals to evaluate and refine procedures for beginning the school day.

THE EDITORIAL COMMITTEE
AGNES KRARUP — *Chairman*

PROGRAMS AND THEMES FOR OPENING EXERCISES

Kindergarten—3

PROGRAMS FOR OPENING EXERCISES

Kindergarten—3

Teachers may choose from these arrangements of the several kinds of materials offered in this resource book, or they are free to develop other combinations according to the needs of their classrooms.

Kindergarten–1

Quiet music: *Song to an Evening Star** by Richard Wagner
Introduction to poem:

The name of that music is "Song to an Evening Star." The evening star is the first one that is seen in the sky when it begins to get dark. Here is a poem about someone who watched the evening star:

FEBRUARY TWILIGHT†

I stood beside a hill
 Smooth with new-laid snow,
A single star looked out
 From the cold evening glow.

There was no other creature
 That saw what I could see
I stood and watched the evening star
 As long as it watched me.

SARA TEASDALE

Introduction to Pledge of Allegiance:

In daylight we cannot see the stars in the sky, but we can see the stars in the American flag. Let us salute our country's flag.

Pledge of Allegiance

◇◇◇◇◇◇◇

* Recording or piano music played by teacher.
† Reprinted with permission of The Macmillan Company from *Stars To-night* by Sara Teasdale. Copyright 1926 by The Macmillan Company, renewed 1954 by Mamie T. Wheless.

Music (for listening only): *Hymn of Joy** by Ludwig van Beethoven
Introduction to the song *Thanksgiving*† by Ethel Crowninshield. (May be used as a song or a poem.)

Here are some things to be thankful for:

Eyes to see and ears to hear;
Feet that will take me far and near;
Little hands to work for me
For all these, I'm glad as I can be.

Minute of silent reflection

During a moment of silence think of some of the things for which you are thankful.

Introduction to Pledge of Allegiance:

We are thankful for our country, the United States of America.
Let us salute the flag of our country.

Pledge of Allegiance

◈◈◈◈◈◈◈

Pledge of Allegiance
Song: *Sing O Sing*** by Satis Coleman and Alice Thorn

Sing, O sing for it is Spring.
Flowers bloom and robins sing.

Introduction to poem:

The first day of spring is in March. The name of the next month is April. Listen to a poem about something that happened the day before April. (Read "The Day Before April"†† by Mary Carolyn Davies.)

---

* From *Our First Music,* Birchard and Company.
† From *Sing a Song* of *The World of Music Series,* copyright, 1936, by Ginn and Company. Used with permission.
** Copyright © by Satis N. Coleman & Alice G. Thorn.
Reprinted from *Singing Time* by Satis N. Coleman & Alice G. Thorn, by permission of The John Day Company, Inc. publisher.
†† From *Very Young Verses,* Barbara Geismer and Antoinette Suter, Houghton Mifflin Company.

Kindergarten–3

Song: *Flag of America**
Pledge of Allegiance
Read aloud:

> I am proud I am an American. I am happy I have my home, my family, my friends, and my school.

Minute of silent reflection

◈◈◈◈◈◈◈

Pledge of Allegiance
First verse of *America*
Poem: *The Flag Goes By* by Henry H. Bennett

> Hats off!
> Along the street there comes
> A blare of bugles, a ruffle of drums,
> A flash of color beneath the sky;
> Hats off!
> The flag is passing by.

Minute of silent reflection

◈◈◈◈◈◈◈

Read pages 4-6 from *Our Country's Flag*† by Georgiady and Romano.
Interpretation and discussion. Reference to illustrations.
Pledge of Allegiance
First verse of *America*
Minute of silent reflection

◈◈◈◈◈◈◈

Grades 2–3

Reading of *A Little Song of Life*** by Lizette Woodworth Reese
Minute of silent reflection
Rereading of last stanza
Pledge of Allegiance
Singing of *America*

◈◈◈◈◈◈◈

---

* From *Twenty Little Songs* by Jessie Carter, Willis Music Company.
† *Our Country's Flag* by Georgiady and Romano, Follett Publishing Company.
** From *Silver Pennies* by Blanche J. Thompson, The Macmillan Company.

Pledge of Allegiance
Singing of *America*
Reading of:

SOMETHING TOLD THE WILD GEESE*

Something told the wild geese
  It was time to go
Though the fields lay golden
  Something whispered, "Snow."
Leaves were green and stirring,
  Berries, luster-glossed,
But beneath warm feathers
  Something whispered, "Frost."
All the sagging orchards
  Steamed with amber spice,
But each wild breast stiffened
  At remembered ice.
Something told the wild geese
  It was time to fly —
Summer sun was on their wings,
  Winter in their cry.

RACHEL FIELD

Minute of silent reflection
Rereading of poem

◈◈◈◈◈◈◈

Pledge of Allegiance
Singing of *America*
Reading of:

NIGHT†

Stars over snow,
  And in the west a planet
Swinging below a star —
  Look for a lovely thing and you will find it,
It is not far —
  It never will be far.

SARA TEASDALE

Discussion of lovely things around
Rereading of poem

◇◇◇◇◇◇◇

First verse of *America*
Pledge of Allegiance
Thought for the day:

A willing helper does not wait until he is asked.

DANISH PROVERB

(This could be written on the board, read aloud by the whole class, then briefly discussed.)

Minute of silent reflection

(Teacher might repeat thought for the day to close meditation period.)

◇◇◇◇◇◇◇

Minute of silent reflection
Pledge of Allegiance
Thought for the day:

We live in deeds, not years.

Prose selection: *The Boy Who Grew Up** by Jay T. Stocking

(The complete reading may take from three to five days. Discussion should follow each day's reading. Values of unselfishness, sharing, and generosity can be stressed.)

◇◇◇◇◇◇◇

The following is an example of a program carried over a ten day period:

Readings to be taken from the book *Abraham Lincoln* by Ingri and Edgar P. d'Aulaire, Doubleday and Company. (The pages are not numbered.) The story may be read in ten readings of three- to four-minute periods.

Program for each morning:

---

* From *Treasured Tales* by Laura Cathon and Thusnelda Schmidt, Abingdon Press.

Reading of part of story
Short discussion of main thought
Pledge of Allegiance

First day

Birth, early childhood and early but brief formal education. Home life is modest and happy. Shows eagerness to learn and to help on the farm. Reading may end with page opposite picture of schoolroom or at end of first paragraph on next page.

Second day

Family moves to Indiana. Abe realizes that things we like best are often hardest to get. Reading ends with story of gingerbread man.

Third day

Death of mother and remarriage of father. Abe shows leadership at early age and great desire for learning. Travels far to borrow books. Encouraged by stepmother. Reading ends with page on which picture shows Abe playing joke on stepmother.

Fourth day

Abe's first trip down the Ohio and Mississippi rivers to New Orleans. Encounter with slavery and deep hurt about it. Reading ends with next to last paragraph of page opposite picture of slaves being sold.

Fifth day

Family moves to Illinois. Abe leaves home to try his luck. Is respected for his humor, kindliness, and honesty. Is nicknamed "Honest Abe." Reading ends with first paragraph opposite picture of Indian hiding behind Abe.

Sixth day

Abe is elected as state representative and studies law. Friends encourage him to make speeches because they are impressed with his concern about humanity and with his brilliant oratory. Abe is too poor to go to school, but his desire to become a lawyer is so great that he studies on his own. Reading ends with page opposite picture of Abe lying on a counter reading a book.

Seventh day

Abe becomes a lawyer and moves to Springfield, Illinois. Marries Mary Todd. Is successful because of his fairness and clever wit. Reading ends with observation, "Abe, you can even make a cat laugh."

Eighth day

Abe is sent to Congress. Returns to Springfield after term is over. Debates with Judge Douglas. Is elected President because of his sincerity and courage to exclaim, "All men are created equal" and "A house divided against itself cannot stand." Reading ends with page opposite picture of Abe going to Washington as President.

Ninth day

The South secedes. Civil War begins. Gettysburg Address. Abe loved peace, but believed that his country could be great only so long as the states were united as one country. Reading ends with page opposite picture of Abe on a horse.

Tenth day

Emancipation Proclamation. End of the Civil War. Abe saved the Union. The slaves were freed.

THEMES FOR OPENING EXERCISES

Patriotic Values

Our flag — meaning, history, respect, displaying
Pledge of Allegiance
National anthem
Places — Capitol, White House, Statue of Liberty
Persons — Abraham Lincoln, Washington, Daniel Boone
Quotations — Nathan Hale, Patrick Henry, John Paul Jones
World friendship

Character Values

Desirable qualities that aid in:

Getting along with other people
Being a good citizen

Becoming a good student
Being a good friend
Being a good member of home and family

Aesthetic Values

Nature
Sense of wonder
Beauty of sounds
Color in the world about us
Magic of words

Some Suitable Aesop's Fables

Tortoise and the Ducks
Belling the Cat
Fox and the Grapes
Lion and the Mouse
Shepherd Boy and the Wolf
Plane Tree
Farmer and the Stork
Travelers and the Purse
Oak and the Seeds
Ants and the Grasshopper
Dog in the Manger
Goose and the Golden Eggs
Dog and His Reflection
Hare and the Tortoise
Fox and the Crow
North Wind and the Sun

PROGRAMS AND THEMES FOR OPENING EXERCISES

Grades 4—6

PROGRAMS FOR OPENING EXERCISES

Grades 4–6

Teachers may choose from these arrangements of the kinds of materials offered in this resource book, or they are free to develop other combinations according to the needs of their classrooms.

First verse of *America*
Pledge of Allegiance
Read aloud:

THE ARROW AND THE SONG

I shot an arrow into the air,
It fell to earth, I know not where;
For, so swiftly it flew, the sight
Could not follow it in its flight.

I breathed a song into the air,
It fell to earth, I know not where;
For who has sight so keen and strong,
That it can follow the flight of song?

Long, long afterward, in an oak
I found the arrow, still unbroke;
And the song, from beginning to end,
I found again in the heart of a friend.

HENRY WADSWORTH LONGFELLOW

Minute of silent reflection
Close meditation with the last stanza of the poem:

Long, long afterward, in an oak
I found the arrow, still unbroke;
And the song, from beginning to end,
I found again in the heart of a friend.

◇◇◇◇◇◇◇

Minute of silent reflection
Pledge of Allegiance
Singing of *The Star-Spangled Banner*
Read aloud:

NOW

If you have hard work to do,
Do it now.
Today the skies are clear and blue,
Tomorrow clouds may come in view,
Yesterday is not for you —
Do it now.

If you have a song to sing,
Sing it now.
Let the notes of gladness ring
Clear as song of bird in spring,
Let every day some music bring —
Sing it now.

If you have kind words to say,
Say them now.
Tomorrow may not come your way,
Do a kindness while you may,
Loved ones will not always stay —
Say them now.

If you have a smile to show,
Show it now.
Make hearts happy, roses grow,
Let the friends around you know
The love you have before they go —
Show it now.

ANONYMOUS

Children's comments on the above poem

◈◈◈◈◈◈◈

Pledge of Allegiance
Sing *God Bless America*
Read aloud:

> We hold these truths to be self-evident, that all men are created equal, that they are endowed by their Creator with certain unalienable Rights, that among these are Life, Liberty and the pursuit of Happiness. That to secure these rights, Governments are instituted among Men, deriving their just powers from the consent of the governed.

DECLARATION OF INDEPENDENCE

Minute of silent reflection

◈◈◈◈◈◈◈

Pledge of Allegiance
First verse of *America the Beautiful*
Quotation:

> I hope to find my country in the right: however
> I will stand by her, right or wrong.
>
> JOHN J. CRITTENDEN

Minute of silent reflection
Brief discussion concerning the above quotation

◈◈◈◈◈◈◈

Pledge of Allegiance
A reading from the book *America Is My Country*.* It includes symbols of our democracy, our national documents, our monuments and shrines, our patriotic songs, poems, and holidays.
Minute of silent reflection
Singing of *This Is My Country*

List of Suitable Activities

Memorization of:
- American Creed
- Freedom Pledge
- Pledge of Allegiance
- Other stanzas than the well-known first stanza of certain patriotic songs.

Choral speaking.

Discussion and use of all verses of *America, Battle Hymn of the Republic, Columbia, the Gem of the Ocean, America the Beautiful, The Star-Spangled Banner,* etc.

Use of a variety of materials, presented in a meaningful way decided by the teacher or jointly by the teacher and the pupils. It is suggested that the teacher be alert to opportunities that arise from time to time in the classroom, school, home, or community that may lead into an appropriate subject for opening exercises. This may call for adapting from a preconceived plan to one to take advantage of the opportunity.

Thought for the day written on the board.

Statement about a holiday or special occasion written by a committee.

---

* *America Is My Country* by Brown and Guadagnolo, Houghton Mifflin Company.

One prose selection continued each morning until concluded (in serial form not more than one week).

Reading of selections from books, newspapers, and magazines brought to school by the children.

Events of historical significance and birthdays of famous people which occur in a particular month could be discussed.

Each child could be assigned a date which has some significance in a particular month. Using library references, children could prepare for their particular days; then of each special day, tell in a few sentences about it. After this, the teacher may read a poem of some historical significance appropriate to the fact given.

THEMES FOR OPENING EXERCISES

Patriotic Values

- Our Presidents
- Famous Americans
- Our Constitution
- Our flag and its meaning
- Watchwords of liberty (quotations)
- Songs of our land
- Statue of Liberty
- The Liberty Bell and Independence Hall
- Patriotic symbols
  - American flag
  - Eagle
  - Uncle Sam
  - Monuments
- Getting acquainted with the Capitol
- Getting acquainted with the White House
- Brotherhood

Understandings

- Our responsibilities toward one another
- Our responsibilities to our home and family
- Our responsibilities to our school
- Our responsibilities as American citizens
- Our responsibilities as citizens of the world

PROGRAMS AND THEMES FOR OPENING EXERCISES

Grades 7—9

PROGRAMS FOR OPENING EXERCISES

Grades 7—9

Teachers may choose from these arrangements of the kinds of materials offered in this resource book, or they are free to develop other combinations according to the needs of their classrooms. The reading of the bulletin and the marking of the roll are assumed to be a part of morning exercises but are omitted from the formats listed below.

Pledge of Allegiance
Reading or presentation of excerpt
Minute of silent reflection

◈◈◈◈◈◈◈

Group singing of a patriotic song, e.g., the national anthem, *My Country 'Tis of Thee, God Bless America, America The Beautiful*
or
Broadcasting all or a portion of a recorded patriotic song to all rooms over the P. A. system
Reading or presentation of excerpt
Minute of silent reflection
Pledge of Allegiance

◈◈◈◈◈◈◈

Broadcasting of patriotic or serious music over P. A. system
or
Listening to an excerpt of serious music broadcast within a classroom
Minute of silent reflection
Pledge of Allegiance

◈◈◈◈◈◈◈

Pledge of Allegiance
Reading of excerpt by pupil (properly prepared)
Minute of silent reflection

◈◈◈◈◈◈◈

Pledge of Allegiance
Viewing of picture of artistic value from overhead projector with brief but appropriate comment by teacher
Minute of silent reflection

Pledge of Allegiance
Projection of quotation using an overhead projector
or
Group reading of quotation
or
Responsive reading of a quotation
Minute of silent reflection

> Every voter as surely as your public magistrate exercises a public trust.
>
> GROVER CLEVELAND

> I go for all sharing the privileges of the government who assist in bearing its burdens. Consequently I go for admitting all to the right to vote who pay taxes or bear arms.
>
> ABRAHAM LINCOLN

VOTE TODAY

Group singing of America

◈◈◈◈◈◈◈

Ralph Waldo Emerson, American thinker and essayist, has contributed many wise sayings that have passed into our common stock of quotations:

> I trust a good deal to common fame as we all must. If a man has good corn, or wood, or boards, or pigs, to sell, or can make better chairs or knives, crucibles, or church organs, than anybody else, you will find a broad, hardbeaten road to his house, though it be in the woods.

Here is the idea in briefer form as you have probably heard it:

> If you write a better book, or preach a better sermon, or build a better mousetrap than your neighbor, the world will make a beaten track to your door.

Pledge of Allegiance

◈◈◈◈◈◈◈

Samples of materials that can be used during a three-week period:

Halloween

First day

The last week in October has long been regarded as the end of summer and early fall, the beginning of the late fall and winter seasons. It marks the change to different physical activities and, with Halloween, the beginning of different social activities. It is the time for making plans, for self-appraisal, for reflective thinking.

It has been said that the art of thinking is the greatest art of all, for "as a man thinketh in his heart, so is he."

Second day

Yesterday we read that "as a man thinketh in his heart, so is he."

That means, of course, that one gradually becomes what he habitually thinks. Josiah Gilbert Holland expressed it like this:

Heaven is not reached at a single bound;
But we build the ladder by which we rise
From the lowly earth to the vaulted skies
And we mount to its summit round by round.

Third day

It has been said that we are the product of our thinking and of our heritage. This is illustrated by our observation of Halloween.

Halloween was first observed long before the birth of Christ by a people called the Celts, who lived in the British Isles and northern France. They feared that when winter came, the sun they worshiped would be killed by the powers of darkness. They tried to save their god by paying a sort of tax to the forces of evil in a great ceremony on the night that we know as Halloween. They burned some of their crops and animals in huge fires, hoping this would please the evil powers so that they would let the sun come back.

Of course modern people know that the sun always returns. Only a few weeks after Halloween, on December 21, the days begin to grow longer, and very slowly but surely, the days begin to get warmer. The Celts, who did not know how the earth moves about the sun, thought this was because the powers of darkness had accepted their sacrifices on Halloween.

Fourth day

Yesterday we read of the early Celts and their observation of Halloween. There are many other reminders of this practice.

The black cat that decorates your Halloween parties is there because the Celts believed all the spirits of the dead were called together on the night of Halloween. A sort of court was held then by the Lord of Death, who decided what form the spirits would take during the following year. Wicked spirits had to take the form of cats. Because of this, people were afraid of cats. They believed cats had evil powers.

Christians did everything they could to change these old beliefs about the evening of October 31. The Roman Catholic Church set aside the first day of November to honor all the saints who had no special days of their own. This day became known as All Saints' Day, and the night before it was called Allhallow Eve. This was shortened to Halloween. And after many hundreds of years, people stopped believing in witches and the powers of darkness.

Fifth day

For a long time there was still another belief in many countries about this mysterious night. It was the belief that between sunset and sunrise on Halloween the spirits of the dead were free to walk about the earth. When you wrap a sheet around yourself on Halloween and pretend to be a ghost, or dress in a costume that looks like a skeleton, with a skull for a mask, you probably resemble very closely the idea of what dead souls looked like.

The dead were very much in the thoughts of the living on Halloween. Families visited graves or churches to pray that the dead would rest in peace. And in England a very curious custom grew up. It was called "going asouling." Men and women went about from house to house calling:

"A soulcake, a soulcake
A penny or a soulcake!"

Housewives gave them little pastries called soulcakes, and in return they said prayers for the souls of the dead.

Today most children dress up and go around on Halloween saying at each door, "Trick or treat!"

Election Day

First day

Tomorrow is Election Day, a day when citizens all over America go to the polls to choose men to carry on the work of the government. The kind of public officials we seek is described in these lines from a poem by Josiah Holland (see also page 102).

> God, give us men! A time like this demands
> Strong minds, great hearts, true faith, and ready hands;
> Men whom the lust of office does not kill;
> Men whom the spoils of office cannot buy;
> Men who possess opinions and a will;
> Men who have honor; men who will not lie . . .

Second day

Today there will be many citizens who will fail to exercise the privilege and duty of voting. They feel that one vote is not important. But —

Thomas Jefferson was elected President by just one vote in the Electoral College. So was John Quincy Adams. Rutherford B. Hayes was elected President by just one vote. His election was contested and referred to an electoral commission. Again he won by a single vote. The man who cast that deciding vote for President Hayes was a lawyer from Indiana who was elected to Congress by the margin of just one vote. That one vote was cast by a client of his who, though desperately ill, insisted on being taken to the polls to cast that one vote.

Veterans Day

First day

November 11 is Veterans Day. This holiday has been celebrated since 1918, although it was not always called Veterans Day. Originally it was called Armistice Day, commemorating the agreement which ended hostilities in World War I. Every year our nation paid tribute to the servicemen of that war and, later, to those of the Second World War. Finally, in 1954, Congress changed the name to Veterans Day to honor those who fought in all our country's wars.

It is traditional to observe a minute of silence at 11 a.m. on Veterans Day. In the words of General Pershing:

> We pay silent and grateful tribute today to those gallant sons of America who have given their lives that the great principles of liberty and justice might endure.

Second day

More than a hundred years ago, in his poem *Locksley Hall,* Alfred Tennyson prophesied the horror of aerial warfare. Let us hope that his vision of universal law and order, found in the same poem, will prove as prophetic.

For I dipped into the future, far as human eye could
  see,
Saw the vision of the world, and all the wonder that
  would be;

Saw the heavens fill with commerce, argosies of magic
  sails,
Pilots of the purple twilight, dropping down with
  costly bales;

Saw the heavens fill with shouting, and there rained
  a ghastly dew,
From the nations' airy navies grappling in the central
  blue;

Far along the world-wide whisper of the south wind
  rushing warm,
With the standards of the peoples plunging through
  the thunderstorm;

Till the war drum throbbed no longer, and the battle
  flags were furled,
In the parliament of man, the federation of the world.

There the common sense of most shall hold a fretful
  realm in awe,
And the kindly earth shall slumber, lapped in universal
  law.

Third day

On Veterans Day, when we pause to honor those who have given their lives in our country's wars, it is good for us to consider that warfare is evidence that we are not yet fully civilized, and to try to raise ourselves to that level of civilization where the use of force between nations will be obsolete.

Henry Wadsworth Longfellow expresses something of this in his poem "The Arsenal at Springfield."

> Were half the power that fill the world with terror,
> Were half the wealth bestowed on camps and courts,
> Given to redeem the human mind from error,
> There were no need for arsenals nor forts.
>
> The warrior's name would be a name abhorred!
> And every nation that should lift again
> Its hand against a brother, on its forehead
> Would wear forevermore the curse of Cain!

Thanksgiving Day

First day

Thanksgiving Day was officially announced as a legal annual holiday in 1863. In October of that year in the midst of the Civil War, Abraham Lincoln issued a National Thanksgiving Proclamation establishing the event with these opening words:

> The year that is drawing toward its close has been filled with the blessings of fruitful fields and healthful skies. To these bounties, which are so constantly enjoyed that we are prone to forget the source from which they come, others have been added, which are of so extraordinary a nature that they cannot fail to penetrate and soften the heart which is habitually insensible to the ever-watchful providence of Almighty God.

Second day

One reason that makes the Thanksgiving festivity so meaningful to Americans is the fact that many items of the first Thanksgiving are still served on today's tables.

The domesticated turkeys of today are not direct descendants of the small wild turkeys in 1621, but they are thoroughly American with a remarkable history of world travels.

One of the more advanced Indian civilizations, the Aztecs in Central America, had tamed a wild turkey species which the conquering Spaniards seized and carried home to Spain. At that time, Spaniards were trading with Mohammedans who held the southern coast of the Mediterranean. The birds were carried to the two great Moslem centers, Mecca and Turkey.

From the latter place, they were shipped through the lower Danube Valley. Eventually, they turned up in Austria and Germany, then France and England, and finally back again on American shores.

Many Europeans thought the birds originated in Turkey and hence gave them that name.

Both Benjamin Franklin and John James Audubon felt that the small, bright-eyed wild turkey should be elevated to the status of the national symbol instead of the American eagle.

Philosophical Thoughts From Some of the World's Great Religions

First day

Leaders of all of the world's great religions have emphasized in their teaching and in their writing strikingly similar ideals of human behavior. After hearing these daily readings, perhaps you will recognize some parallels.

Lao-tse, who lived in China in the sixth century B.C., is the author of this reading:

> I have three treasures which I hold and keep safe:
> The first is called love;
> The second is called moderation;
> The third is called not venturing to go ahead of the world.
> Being loving, one can be brave;
> Being moderate, one can be ample;
> Not venturing to go ahead of the world, one can be the chief
> of all officials.
> For he who fights with love will win the battle;
> He who defends with love will be secure.
> Heaven will save him, and protect him with love.

Second day

Confucius, a wise and good teacher who lived in China about five hundred years before Christ, left a series of precepts or rules of behavior. Here are three of them:

> The princely man thinks of virtue; the mean man of gain.
>
> The real fault is to have faults and not try to amend them.
>
> Do not unto others what you do not like done unto yourself.

Gautama Buddha gave up the luxurious life of a prince in India some five hundred years before Jesus to seek a holy life. He founded Buddhism, which is the chief religion of Southeast Asia today. He said:

> All that we are is the result of what we have thought; it is founded on our thoughts; it is made up of our thoughts. If a man speaks or acts with a pure thought, happiness follows him, like a shadow that never leaves him.

Third day

Judaism holds that man can most genuinely worship God by imitating those qualities that are godly: As God is merciful, so must we be compassionate; as God is just, so must we deal justly with our neighbor; as God is slow to anger, so must we be tolerant.

The three basic principles of faith are (1) love of learning, (2) worship of God, (3) good deeds.

> Hear, O Israel: The Lord our God, the Lord is one. And thou shalt love the Lord thy God with all thy heart, with all thy soul, and with all thy might.
>
> DEUTERONOMY 6:4-5

> Thou shalt not hate thy brother in thine heart. Thou shalt not avenge, nor bear any grudge against the children of thy people, but shalt love thy neighbor as thyself: I am the Lord.
>
> LEVITICUS 19:17-18

> . . . what doth the Lord require of thee, but to do justly, and to love mercy, and to walk humbly with thy God?
>
> MICAH 6:8

Fourth day

In the New Testament, the words of Jesus, as spoken in the Sermon on the Mount:

> But I say unto you which hear, Love your enemies, do good to them which hate you,
>
> Bless them that curse you, and pray for them which despitefully use you.
>
> And unto him that smiteth thee on the one cheek offer also the other; and him that taketh away thy cloak forbid not to take the coat also.
>
> Give to every man that asketh of thee; and of him that taketh away thy goods ask them not again.
>
> And as ye would that men should do to you, do ye also to them likewise.

Fifth day

In the sixth century A.D., Mohammed founded in Arabia the religion of Islam, often mistakenly called Mohammedanism. The Koran, the holy book of his followers, the Muslims, contains in its opening chapter these words, which are recited by every Muslim five times each day:

> Praise belongs to God, Lord of the Worlds,
> The Compassionate, the Merciful
> King of the day of Judgment.
> 'Tis Thee we worship and Thee we ask for help.
> Guide us in the straight path,
> The path of those whom Thou hast favored,
> Not the path of those who incur Thine anger nor
> of those who go astray.

List of Suitable Activities

Reading of an excerpt properly introduced by teacher.

Prepared reading by a pupil.

Responsive reading for purpose of emotional impact, understanding and learning, e.g., *America the Beautiful.*

Reading in unison, e.g., Gettysburg Address.

Presentation of material prepared by student committees.

Pupil or teacher preparation and discussion of bulletin board displays based upon the current theme or various inspirational thoughts.

Thoughtful consideration of a picture, e.g., a Gothic cathedral, or stained-glass windows by Chagall.

Silent reading of an excerpt, with or without discussion.

Group listening to recorded music, e.g. *New World Symphony,* 2nd movement, by Dvorak.

Group singing accompanied by piano, record player, or possibly broadcast over the public-address system.

Attractive presentation of the thought for the day or week on blackboard or bulletin board.

Group listening to special programs presented over the public-address system.

Group listening to special programs written by staff members or pupils

Group recitation of school code.

Group singing of the school's alma mater.

THEMES FOR OPENING EXERCISES

Character Values

Appreciation of home
Appreciation of school
Cooperation
Fair play
Individuality
Participation
Self-discipline
Self-respect
Sharing

Patriotic Values

Appreciation of country
Civic pride
Civil liberties
Civil obedience
Effective citizenship
Law enforcement
Responsibility to self
Responsibility to others
People of America

Ethical Values

Spiritual growth
Integrity
Moral development
Interreligious understanding
Intergroup understanding

Aesthetic Values

Civic pride — beauty of old and new buildings
Beauty of nature
Beauty in literature
Beauty in music
Beauty in painting

PROGRAMS AND THEMES FOR OPENING EXERCISES

Grades 10–12

PROGRAMS FOR OPENING EXERCISES

Grades 10—12

Teachers may choose from these arrangements of the kinds of materials offered in this resource book, or they are free to develop other combinations according to the needs of their classrooms. The reading of the bulletin and the marking of the roll are assumed to be a part of morning exercises but are omitted from the format listed below.

Music: "Trio in A Minor" by Maurice Ravel
Reading for the day:

WHY ARE YOU IN SCHOOL?

. . . To seek intellectual growth.
. . . To ask questions; to discover the answers by thinking.
. . . To master the basic tools and to use your learning.
Become interested in modern man's inheritance from the past — literature, art, history, music.
. . . Learn values — the values of citizenship, of freedom, or honor, or integrity; qualities that will make a safe and sane world.
. . . Learn to work as hard as you can.
. . . Develop habits of rational thinking and problem solving.
. . . Develop your body and your mind.
. . . Discover beauty.
. . . Develop a respect for hard work and a responsibility for its complete accomplishment.
. . . MOST IMPORTANT OF ALL: become aware of moral and spiritual values; develop a sense of purpose beyond mere existence.

SIDNEY P. MARLAND, JR.*

Pledge of Allegiance

◈◈◈◈◈◈◈

MESSAGE TO THE BOYS OF AMERICA

Of course what we have a right to expect from the American boy is that he shall turn out to be a good American man. Now, the chances are strong that he WON'T be much of a man unless he is a good deal of a boy. He must NOT be a coward or a weakling, a bully, a shirk, or a prig.

* Superintendent of Schools, Pittsburgh.

He must work hard and play hard. He must be clean-minded and clean-lived, and able to hold his own under all circumstances and against all comers. It is only on these conditions that he will grow into the kind of man of whom America can really be proud. In life, as in a football game, the principle to follow is:

HIT THE LINE HARD
DON'T FOUL AND DON'T SHIRK
BUT HIT . . . THE . . . LINE . . . HARD.

THEODORE ROOSEVELT

Pledge of Allegiance

◈◈◈◈◈◈◈

Good morning! Let us rise for the national anthem, and remain standing at its close for the Pledge of Allegiance to the flag. (Music) "I pledge allegiance to the flag of the United States of America . . ." (Completion of Pledge)

Since football is opening our fall season of sports, and we play today, this is an appropriate time to think about sportsmanship. Here is a definition for us to consider, and to follow today. "Sportmanship is playing hard to win in every game, but losing well if you have to lose. Good sportsmanship involves such matters as fair play, keen rivalry, and, at the same time, the careful observance of rules, genuine courtesy, and a generous attitude toward an opponent."

And now, the bulletin for today (give date) . . . (reading of bulletin).

◈◈◈◈◈◈◈

Good morning . . . through Pledge.

Today begins more than a week of the most important holidays for persons of Jewish faith. They culminate in the holiday, Yom Kippur. Yom Kippur is known as "The Day of Atonement." On this day the devout Jew thinks of his sins, repents, and asks God for forgiveness. Most modern Jews celebrate it by fasting from sunset to sunset, by doing no work, and by attending services in the synagogue or temple. This is also the season of the beginning of the New Year on the ancient Jewish calendar, and an appropriate time to wish your Jewish friends "Happy New Year."

Bulletin, etc.

◈◈◈◈◈◈◈

Here is an example of a program carried over three days:

First day

The fate of any member of a group — your family, your school, your neighborhood, your nation, even the human race — affects all the members of that group. This is not a new idea. Three hundred years ago an English clergyman and poet — John Donne — felt and expressed this same profound thought (see also page 104).

> No man is an island, entire of itself;
> Every man is a piece of the continent, a part of the main;
> If a clod be washed away by the sea, Europe is the less,
> As well as if a promontory were,
> As well as if a manor of thy friend's or of thine own were;
> Any man's death diminishes me,
> Because I am involved in mankind;
> And therefore never send to know for whom the bell tolls;
> It tolls for thee.

Second day

All nations and races have had their wise men who taught the importance of upright behavior and good character in the individual. One of these wise men was a great Chinese philosopher who, more than two thousand years ago, uttered these words:

> With righteousness in the heart, there will be beauty in the character;
> With beauty in the character, there will be harmony in the home;
> With harmony in the home, there will be order in the nation;
> And with order in the nation, there will be peace in the world.

Third day

Our reading comes from Carl Schurz, who as a young and idealistic university student fled from Germany after an unsuccessful fight for democracy in that country. Settling in America, he became a statesman and a friend of Lincoln's. This poetic statement is often quoted and is short enough to be memorized:

> Ideals are like the stars — we never reach them,
> but like the mariners on the sea, we chart our
> courses by them.

List of Suitable Activities

Pledge of Allegiance

Minute of silent reflection

Inspirational music

Choral speaking

Readings

- Poems
- Essays
- Biographies or journals
- Inscriptions
- Description of historical events
- Speeches or addresses
- Original themes

THEMES FOR OPENING EXERCISES

Patriotic Values

- Civic responsibilities
- Civil liberties
- Democracy
- Freedom
- International amity
- Peace

Personal Philosophy

- Brotherhood
- Integrity
- Self-realization
- Service

Aesthetic Appreciation

- Appreciation of great books
- Appreciation of nature
- Art, the universal language
- Poetry, the expression of beauty
- Preservation of public property
- Well-known themes from classical music

POETRY AND PROSE SELECTIONS

Arranged by Groups in
Ascending Order of Difficulty

POETRY AND PROSE

Grades K–3

WHO HAS SEEN THE WIND?

Who has seen the wind?
  Neither I nor you:
But when the leaves hang trembling,
  The wind is passing through.

Who has seen the wind?
  Neither you nor I:
But when the trees bow down their heads,
  The wind is passing by.

CHRISTINA GEORGINA ROSSETTI

THE WIND

I saw you toss the kites on high
And blow the birds about the sky;
And all around I heard you pass,
Like ladies' skirts across the grass —
  O wind, a-blowing all day long,
  O wind, that sings so loud a song!

I saw the different things you did,
But always you yourself you hid.
I felt you push, I heard you call,
I could not see yourself at all —
  O wind, a-blowing all day long,
  O wind, that sings so loud a song!

O you that are so strong and cold,
O blower, are you young or old?
Are you a beast of field and tree,
Or just a stronger child than me?
  O wind, a-blowing all day long,
  O wind, that sings so loud a song!

ROBERT LOUIS STEVENSON

BOATS

Boats sail on the rivers,
  And ships sail on the seas;
But clouds that sail across the sky
  Are prettier far than these.

There are bridges on the rivers,
  As pretty as you please;
But the bow that bridges heaven,
  And overtops the trees,
And builds a road from earth to sky,
  Is prettier far than these.

CHRISTINA GEORGINA ROSSETTI

FALLING SNOW

See the pretty snowflakes
  Falling from the sky;
On the walk and housetop
  Soft and thick they lie.

On the window-ledges
  On the branches bare;
Now how fast they gather,
  Filling all the air.

Look into the garden,
  Where the grass was green;
Covered by the snowflakes,
  Not a blade is seen.

Now the bare black bushes
  All look soft and white,
Every twig is laden —
  What a pretty sight!

ANONYMOUS

◈◈◈

"When we work and play together
In a kind and friendly way
Taking turns and sharing playthings
We will have a happy day."

ANONYMOUS

A GOOD BOY

I woke before the morning,
  I was happy all the day.
I never said an ugly word,
  But smiled and stuck to play.
And now at last the sun
  Is going down behind the wood,
And I am very happy,
  For I know that I've been good.

ROBERT LOUIS STEVENSON

SONG

The year's at the spring,
And day's at the morn;
Morning's at seven;
The hillside's dew-pearled;
The lark's on the wing;
The snail's on the thorn;
God's in His Heaven —
All's right with the world!

ROBERT BROWNING

THE SUN IS UP

The lark is up to greet the sun,
The bee is on the wing;
The ant its labor has begun,
The woods with music ring.

JANE TAYLOR

OUT IN THE FIELDS WITH GOD

The little cares that fretted me
I lost them yesterday
Among the fields, above the sea,
Among the winds at play,
Among the lowing of the herds,
The rustling of the trees,
Among the singing of the birds,
The humming of the bees.

The foolish fears of what might happen,
I cast them all away,
Among the clover-scented grass,
Among the new-mown hay,
Among the husking of the corn,
Where drowsy poppies nod,
Where ill thoughts die and good are born —
Out in the fields with God.

Attributed to Elizabeth Barrett Browning

THE STAR

Twinkle, twinkle, little star,
How I wonder what you are,
Up above the world so high,
Like a diamond in the sky.

When the blazing sun is set,
And the grass with dew is wet,
Then you show your little light,
Twinkle, twinkle, all the night.

Then the traveler in the dark
Thanks you for your tiny spark,
He could not see where to go
If you did not twinkle so.

In the dark blue sky you keep,
And often through my curtains peep,
For you never shut your eye
Till the sun is in the sky.

As your bright and tiny spark
Lights the traveler in the dark,
Though I know not what you are,
Twinkle, twinkle, little star.

Jane Taylor

THREE THINGS TO REMEMBER

A Robin Redbreast in a cage
Puts all Heaven in a rage.

A skylark wounded on the wing
Doth make a cherub cease to sing.

He who shall hurt the little wren
Shall never be beloved by men.

William Blake

THE SUN'S TRAVELS

The sun is not abed, when I
At night upon my pillow lie;
Still round the earth his way he takes,
And morning after morning makes.

While here at home, in shining day,
We round the sunny garden play,
Each little Indian sleepyhead
Is being kissed and put to bed.

And when at eve I rise from tea,
Day dawns beyond the Atlantic Sea;
And all the children in the West
Are getting up and being dressed.

Robert Louis Stevenson

THE CHICKADEE

Piped a tiny voice hard by,
Gay and polite, a cheerful cry,
"Chic-chicadee-dee!" Saucy note
Out of a sound heart and a merry throat,
As if it said, "Good day, good sir.
Fine afternoon, old passenger!
Happy to meet you in these places
When January brings new faces!"

Ralph Waldo Emerson

OH, FAIR TO SEE

Oh, fair to see
Bloom-laden cherry tree,
  Arrayed in sunny white:
  An April day's delight,
Oh, fair to see!

Oh, fair to see
Fruit-laden cherry tree,
With balls of shining red
Decking a leafy head,
Oh, fair to see!

CHRISTINA GEORGINA ROSSETTI

HOW DOTH THE LITTLE BUSY BEE

How doth the little busy bee
Improve each shining hour,
And gather honey all the day
From every opening flower!

How skillfully she builds her cell!
How neat she spreads the wax!
And labours hard to store it well
With the sweet food she makes.

ISAAC WATTS

SEPTEMBER

The goldenrod is yellow;
The corn is turning brown;
The trees in apple orchards
With fruit are bending down.

The gentian's bluest fringes
Are curling in the sun;
In dusty pods the milkweed
Its hidden silk has spun.

The sedges flaunt their harvest
In every meadow nook;
And asters by the brook-side
Make asters in the brook.

From dewy lanes at morning
The grapes' sweet odors rise;
At noon the roads all flutter
With yellow butterflies.

By all these lovely tokens
September days are here,
With summer's best of weather,
And autumn's best of cheer.

HELEN HUNT JACKSON

LITTLE THINGS

Little drops of water,
Little grains of sand,
Make the mighty ocean
And the pleasant land.

Little deeds of kindness,
Little words of love,
Help to make earth happy
Like the heaven above.

JULIA A. F. CARNEY

HURT NO LIVING THING

Hurt no living thing:
Ladybird, no butterfly,
Nor moth with dusty wing,
No cricket chirping cheerily,
Nor grasshopper so light of leap,
Nor dancing gnat, no beetle fat,
Nor harmless worms that creep.

CHRISTINA GEORGINA ROSSETTI

CHILD'S GRACE*

I give thanks for the lovely-colored year,
For the marigold sun and the slanting silver rain,
For feathery snow across the hemlock hills,
For the sailing moon twelve times grown full again.

I give thanks for my family: Father, Mother,
And all the happy things we do together;
For understanding, laughter, and for love
Strong and warm in any kind of weather.

FRANCES FROST

---

* From *The Little Whistler* by Frances Frost. Copyright 1949 by McGraw-Hill, Inc. Used by permission of McGraw-Hill Book Company.

A WISH IS QUITE A TINY THING*

A wish is quite a tiny thing
Just like a bird upon the wing,
It flies away all fancy free
And lights upon a house or tree;
It flies across the farthest air,
And builds a safe nest anywhere.

ANNETTE WYNNE

KINDNESS TO ANIMALS

Little children, never give
Pain to things that feel and live;
Let the gentle robin come
For the crumbs you save at home, —
As his meat you throw along
He'll repay you with a song;
Never hurt the timid hare
Peeping from her green grass lair,
Let her come and sport and play
On the lawn at close of day;
The little lark goes soaring high
To the bright windows of the sky,
Singing as if 'twere always spring,
And fluttering on an untired wing, —
Oh! let him sing his happy song,
Nor do these gentle creatures wrong.

ANONYMOUS

THE HAPPY WORLD

The bee is a rover;
  The brown bee is gay;
To feed on the clover,
  He passes this way.

Brown bee, humming over,
  What is it you say?
"The world is so happy — so happy
  today!"

WILLIAM BRIGHTY RANDS

REMEMBERING DAY

All the soldiers marching along;
All the children singing a song;
All the flowers dewy and sweet;
All the flags hung out in the street;
Hearts that throb in a grateful way —
For this is our Remembering Day.

MARY WRIGHT SAUNDERS

I'M GLAD

I'm glad the sky is painted blue,
And the earth is painted green,
With such a lot of nice fresh air
All sandwiched in between.

ANONYMOUS

ROBIN

Robin sang sweetly
When the days were bright:
"Thanks, thanks for summer,"
He sang with all his might.

Robin sang sweetly,
In the autumn days,
"There are fruits for everyone;
Let all give praise."

In the cold and wintry weather,
Still hear his song:
"Somebody must sing," said Robin
"Or winter will seem long."

When the spring came back again,
He sang, "I told you so!
Keep on singing through the winter;
It will always go."

ANONYMOUS

THE SECRET

We have a secret, just we three,
The robin, and I, and the sweet cherry-tree;
The bird told the tree, and the tree told me,
And nobody knows it but just us three.

But of course the robin knows it best,
Because he built the — I shan't tell the rest;
And laid the four little — something in it —
I'm afraid I shall tell it every minute.

But if the tree and the robin don't peep,
I'll try my best the secret to keep;
Though I know when the little birds fly about
Then the whole secret will be out.

Anonymous

OUR MOTHER

Hundreds of stars in the pretty sky,
  Hundreds of shells on the shore together,
Hundreds of birds that go singing by,
  Hundreds of birds in the sunny weather,
Hundreds of dewdrops to greet the dawn,
  Hundreds of bees in the purple clover,
Hundreds of butterflies on the lawn,
  But only one mother the wide world over.

Anonymous

ROBIN REDBREAST

Good-by, good-by to Summer!
  For Summer's nearly done;
The garden smiling faintly,
  Cool breezes in the sun;
Our thrushes now are silent,
  Our swallows flown away, —
But Robin's here in coat of brown,
  And scarlet breast-knot gay.
    Robin, Robin Redbreast,
      O Robin dear!
    Robin sings so sweetly
      In the falling of the year.

Bright yellow, red, and orange,
  The leaves come down in hosts;
The trees are Indian princes,
  But soon they'll turn to ghosts;
The scanty pears and apples
  Hang russet on the bough;
It's Autumn, Autumn, Autumn late,
  'Twill soon be Winter now.
    Robin, Robin Redbreast,
      O Robin dear!
    And what will this poor Robin do?
      For pinching days are near.

The fireside for the cricket,
  The wheat-stack for the mouse,
When trembling night-winds whistle
  And moan all round the house.
The frosty ways like iron,
  The branches plumed with snow, —
Alas! in Winter dead and dark,
  Where can poor Robin go?
    Robin, Robin Redbreast,
      O Robin dear!
    And a crumb of bread for Robin,
      His little heart to cheer!

WILLIAM ALLINGHAM

THIS HAPPY DAY*

Every morning when the sun
Comes smiling up on everyone,
It's lots of fun
To say good morning to the sun.
  Good morning, Sun!

Every evening after play
When the sunshine goes away,
It's nice to say,
Thank you for this happy day,
  This happy day!

HARRY BEHN

* From *The Little Hill,* copyright 1949 by Harry Behn. Reprinted by permission of Harcourt, Brace and World, Inc.

TREES*

Trees are the kindest things I know,
They do no harm, they simply grow

And spread a shade for sleepy cows,
And gather birds among their boughs.

They give us fruit in leaves above,
And wood to make our houses of,

And leaves to burn on Hallowe'en,
And in the Spring new buds of green.

They are the first when day's begun
To touch the beams of morning sun,

They are the last to hold the light
When evening changes into night,

And when a moon floats on the sky
They hum a drowsy lullaby

Of sleepy children long ago . . .
Trees are the kindest things I know.

HARRY BEHN

THE BLACKBIRD

In the far corner
Close by the swings,
Every morning
A blackbird sings.

His bill's so yellow,
His coat's so black,
That he makes a fellow
Whistle back.

Ann, my daughter,
Thinks that he
Sings for us two
Especially.

HUMBERT WOLFE

* From *The Little Hill,* copyright 1949 by Harry Behn. Reprinted by permission of Harcourt, Brace and World, Inc.

◈◈◈

For want of a nail
  The shoe was lost,
For want of a shoe
  The horse was lost,
For want of a horse
  The rider was lost,
For want of a rider
  The battle was lost,
For want of a battle
  The kingdom was lost,
And all for the want
  Of a horseshoe nail.

ANONYMOUS

RAIN

The rain is raining all around,
  It falls on field and tree,
It rains on the umbrellas here,
  And on the ships at sea.

ROBERT LOUIS STEVENSON

WISHES*

I wish my eyes were big and blue,
And I had golden curls;
I wish my legs were fatter, too,
Like other little girls'!

I'd love a dimple in my chin;
I wish my mouth were small —
And, oh, the way my teeth fit in
I do not like at all!

But Daddy says he really thinks
That when I get my growth,
I'll look like mother, "Cheer up, Jinks!"
He says, and hugs us both.

How very splendid that would be!
I wonder if it's true —
For mother says that she can see
I'm daddy — through and through!

And they don't look alike one bit;
It's queer as queer can be
That I can look like both and it
Just makes me look like me!

And when I wish my hair would curl
And that my eyes were blue,
My mother says, "No, little girl —
For then you'd not be you!"

EDNA KINGSLEY WALLACE

WE ALL LOVE OUR FLAG*

We all love our flag, the red, white, and blue;
So proudly hold it high, as soldiers do!
See how it waves!
Never let it fall!
The Stars and Stripes, the best flag of all!

Let's all face the flag, the red, white, and blue;
And at attention stand as soldiers do!
Hand on your heart, pledge allegiance to
The Stars and Stripes, the red, white, and blue.

ALICE S. MILLIMAN

AUTUMN FIRES

In the other gardens
   And all up the vale,
From the autumn bonfires
   See the smoke trail!

Pleasant summer over
   And all the summer flowers,
The red fire blazed,
   The grey smoke towers.

* From *The Instructor,* copyright 1960 by F.A. Owen Publishing Company.

Sing a song of seasons!
Something bright in all!
Flowers in the summer,
Fires in the fall!

ROBERT LOUIS STEVENSON

SPRING'S ARRIVAL

All the birds have come again,
Hear the happy chorus!
Robin, bluebird, on the wing,
Thrush and wren this message bring.
Spring will soon come marching in,
Come with joyous singing.

ANONYMOUS

TRY, TRY AGAIN

'Tis a lesson you should heed,
Try, try again;
If a first you don't succeed,
Try, try again;
Then your courage should appear,
For, if you will persevere,
You will conquer, never fear;
Try, try again.

WILLIAM EDWARD HICKSON

BEAUTIFUL

Beautiful faces are they that wear
The light of a pleasant spirit there;
Beautiful hands are they that do
Deeds that are noble, good and true;
Beautiful feet are they that go
Swiftly to lighten another's woe.

ANONYMOUS

OUR LIPS AND EARS

If you your lips would keep from slips,
Five things observe with care:
Of whom you speak, to whom you speak,
And how and when and where.

If you your ears would save from jeers,
These things keep mildly hid:
"Myself" and "I," and "mine" and "my,"
And how "I" do and did.

ANONYMOUS

◈◈◈

The moon was but a chin of gold
  A night or two ago,
And now she turns her perfect face
  Upon the world below.

EMILY DICKINSON

SEPTEMBER

There are twelve months throughout the year
From January to December —
And the primest month of all the twelve
Is the merry month of September!
  Then apples so red
  Hang overhead,
  And nuts, ripe-brown,
  Come showering down
In the bountiful days of September!

There are flowers enough in the summer-time
More flowers than I can remember —
But none with the purple, gold, and red
That dye the flowers of September!
The gorgeous flowers of September!
  And the sun looks through
  A clearer blue,
  And the moon at night
  Sheds a clearer light
On the beautiful flowers of September!

MARY HOWITT

POETRY AND PROSE

Grades 4—6

THE AMERICAN CREED

I believe in the United States of America as a government of the people, by the people, for the people; whose just powers are derived from the consent of the governed; a democracy in a republic; a sovereign nation of many sovereign states, a perfect union, one and inseparable; established upon those principles of freedom, equality, justice, and humanity for which American patriots sacrificed their lives and fortunes.

I therefore believe it is my duty to my country to love it; to support its Constitution; to obey its laws; to respect its flag, and to defend it against all enemies.

WILLIAM TYLER PAGE

From ENDYMION

A thing of beauty is a joy forever:
Its loveliness increases; it will never
Pass into nothingness; but still will keep
A bower quiet for us, and a sleep
Full of sweet dreams, and health, and quiet breathing.

JOHN KEATS

O CAPTAIN! MY CAPTAIN!

O Captain! My Captain! our fearful trip
is done,
The ship has weather'd every rack,
the prize we sought is won,
The port is near, the bells I hear,
the people all exulting,
While follow eyes the steady keel,
the vessel grim and daring;

But O heart! heart! heart!
O the bleeding drops of red,
Where on the deck my Captain lies,
Fallen cold and dead.

O Captain! My Captain! rise up
and hear the bells;
Rise up — for you the flag is flung —
for you the bugle trills,
For you bouquets and ribbon'd
wreaths — for you the shores a-crowding,
For you they call the swaying mass, their eager
faces turning;

Here, Captain! dear father!
This arm beneath your head!
It is some dream that on the deck,
You've fallen cold and dead.

My Captain does not answer, his lips
are pale and still,
My father does not feel my arm,
he has no pulse nor will,
The ship is anchor'd safe and sound, its voyage
closed and done,
From fearful trip the victor ship
comes in with object won;

Exult, O shores! and ring, O bells!
But I, with mournful tread,
Walk the deck my Captain lies,
Fallen cold and dead.

WALT WHITMAN

PREAMBLE TO THE U. S. CONSTITUTION

We, the People of the United States, in Order to form a more perfect Union, establish Justice, insure domestic Tranquility, provide for the common defense, promote the general Welfare, and secure the Blessings of Liberty to ourselves and our Posterity, do ordain and establish this Constitution for the United States of America.

GETTYSBURG ADDRESS, NOVEMBER 19, 1863

Four score and seven years ago our fathers brought forth on this continent a new nation, conceived in liberty, and dedicated to the proposition that all men are created equal.

Now we are engaged in a great civil war, testing whether that nation, or any nation so conceived and so dedicated, can long endure. We are met on a great battlefield of that war. We have come to dedicate a portion of that field as a final resting place for those who here gave their lives that that nation might live. It is altogether fitting and proper that we should do this. But in a larger sense we can not dedicate, we can not consecrate, we can not hallow, this ground. The brave men, living and dead, who struggled here, have consecrated it far above our poor power to add or detract. The world will little note, nor long remember, what we say here; but it can never forget what they did here. It is for us, the living, rather to be dedicated here to be unfinished work which they who fought here have thus far so nobly advanced. It is rather for us to be here dedicated to the great task remaining before us, that from these honored dead we take increased devotion to that cause for which they gave the last full measure of devotion; that we here highly resolve that these dead shall not have died in vain, that this nation, under God, shall have a new birth of freedom, and that government of the people, by the people, for the people shall not perish from the earth.

ABRAHAM LINCOLN

JOY OF LIFE

The sun is careering in glory and might,
'Mid the deep blue sky and the clouds so bright;
The billow is tossing its foam on high,
And the summer breezes go lightly by;
The air and the water dance, glitter, and play —
And why should not I be as merry as they?

The linnet is singing the wild wood through,
The fawn's bounding footsteps skim over the dew,
The butterfly flits round the blossoming tree,
And the cowslip and blue-bell are bent by the bee:
All the creatures that dwell in the forest are gay,
And why should not I be as merry as they?

MARY RUSSELL MITFORD

CONCORD HYMN

By the rude bridge that arched the flood,
Their flag to April's breeze unfurled,
Here once the embattled farmers stood,
And fired the shot heard round the world.

The foe long since in silence slept;
Alike the conqueror silent sleeps;
And Time the ruined bridge has swept
Down the dark stream which seaward creeps.

On this green bank, by this soft stream,
We set today a votive stone;
That memory may their deed redeem,
When, like our sires, our sons are gone.

Spirit, that made those heroes dare
To die, and leave their children free,
Bid Time and Nature gently spare
The shaft we raise to them and thee.

Ralph Waldo Emerson

From AGAINST QUARRELLING AND FIGHTING

Let dogs delight to bark and bite,
For God has made them so;
Let bears and lions growl and fight,
For 'tis their nature, too.

But children, you should never let
Such angry passions rise;
Your little hands were never made
To tear each other's eyes.

Whatever brawls disturb the street,
There should be peace at home;
Where sisters dwell and brothers meet,
Quarrels should never come.

Birds in their little nests agree;
And 'tis a shameful sight,
When children of one family
Fall out, and chide and fight.

Isaac Watts

MOTHER NATURE

Beautiful mother is busy all day,
So busy she neither can sing nor say;
But lovely thoughts, in a ceaseless flow,
Through her eyes, and her ears, and her bosom go —
Motion, sight, and sound, and scent,
Weaving a royal, rich content.

When night is come, and her children sleep,
Beautiful mother her watch doth keep;
With glowing stars in her dusky hair
Down she sits to her music rare;
And her instrument that never fails,
Is the hearts and the throats of her nightingales.

George MacDonald

THE SHIP OF STATE

Thou, too, sail on, O Ship of State!
Sail on, O Union, strong and great!
Humanity with all its fears,
With all the hopes of future years,
Is hanging breathless on thy fate!
We know what Master laid thy keel,
What Workmen wrought thy ribs of steel,
Who made each mast, and sail and rope,
What anvils rang, what hammers beat,
In what a forge and what a heat
Were shaped the anchors of thy hope!
Fear not each sudden sound and shock,
'Tis of the wave and not the rock;
'Tis but the flapping of the sail,
And not a rent made by the gale!
In spite of rock and tempest's roar,
In spite of false lights on the shore,
Sail on, nor fear to breast the sea!
Our hearts, our hopes, are all with thee,
Our hearts, our hopes, our prayers, our tears,
Our faith, triumphant o'er our fears,
Are all with thee, — are all with thee!

Henry Wadsworth Longfellow

From THE CORN SONG

Heap high the farmer's wintry hoard!
Heap high the golden corn!
No richer gift has Autumn poured
From out her lavish horn!

Let other lands, exulting glean
The apple from the pine,
The orange from its glossy green,
The cluster from the vine.

But let the good old crop adorn
The hills our fathers trod;
Still let us, for His golden corn,
Send up our thanks to God!

JOHN GREENLEAF WHITTIER

JACK FROST*

The door was shut, as doors should be,
Before you went to bed last night;
Yet Jack Frost has got in, you see,
And left your window silver white.

He must have waited till you slept;
And not a single word he spoke,
But pencilled o'er the panes and crept
Away again before you woke.

And now you cannot see the hills
Nor fields that stretch beyond the lane;
But there are fairer things than these
His fingers traced on every pane.

Rocks and castles towering high;
Hills and dales and streams and fields;
And knights in armour riding by,
With nodding plumes and shining shields.

---

* From *The Child World* by Gabriel Setoun. Reprinted by permission of The Bodley Head, Limited.

And here are little boats, and there
Big ships with sails spread to the breeze;
And yonder, palm trees waving fair
On islands set in silver seas.

And butterflies with gauzy wings;
And herds of cows and flocks of sheep;
And fruit and flowers and all the things
You see when you are sound asleep.

For creeping softly underneath
The door when all the lights are out,
Jack Frost takes every breath you breathe,
And knows the things you think about.

He paints them on the window pane
In fairy lines with frozen steam;
And when you wake you see again
The lovely things you saw in dream.

GABRIEL SETOUN

From CHRISTMAS BELLS

I heard the bells on Christmas Day
Their old, familiar carols play,
   And wild and sweet
   The words repeat
Of peace on earth, good-will to men!

Then pealed the bells more loud and deep:
"God is not dead; nor doth He sleep!
   The Wrong shall fail,
   The Right prevail,
With peace on earth, good-will to men!"

HENRY WADSWORTH LONGFELLOW

LIKE WASHINGTON

We cannot all be Washingtons,
And have our birthdays celebrated;
But we can love the things he loved,
And we can hate the things he hated.

He loved the truth, he hated lies,
He minded what his mother taught him,
And every day he tried to do
The simple duties that it brought him.

Perhaps the reason little folks
Are sometimes great when they grow taller,
Is just because, like Washington,
They do their best when they are smaller.

ANONYMOUS

TO-DAY

So here hath been dawning
Another blue Day:
Think, wilt thou let it
Slip useless away?

Out of Eternity
This new Day was born;
Into Eternity,
At night, will return.

Behold it aforetime
No eye ever did:
So soon it forever
From all eyes is hid.

Here hath been dawning
Another blue Day:
Think, wilt thou let it
Slip useless away?

THOMAS CARLYLE

OPPORTUNITY

This I beheld, or dreamed it in a dream: —
There spread a cloud of dust along a plain;
And underneath the cloud, or in it, raged
A furious battle, and men yelled, and swords

Shocked upon swords and shields. A prince's banner
Wavered, then staggered backward, hemmed by foes.
A craven hung along the battle's edge,
And thought, "Had I a sword of keener steel —
That blue blade that the king's son bears, — but this
Blunt thing!" he snapt and flung it from his hand,
And lowering crept away and left the field.
Then came the king's son, wounded, sore bestead,
And weaponless, and saw the broken sword,
Hilt-buried in the dry and trodden sand,
And ran and snatched it, and with battle-shout
Lifted afresh he hewed his enemy down,
And saved a great cause that heroic day.

EDWARD ROWLAND SILL

◈◈◈

It sifts from leaden sieves,
It powders all the wood,
It fills with alabaster wool
The wrinkles of the road.

It makes an even face
Of mountain and of plain —
Unbroken forehead from the east
Unto the east again.

It reaches to the fence,
It wraps it, rail by rail,
Till it is lost in fleeces;
It flings a crystal veil.

On stump and stack and stem, —
The summer's empty room,
Acres of seams where harvests were,
Recordless, but for them.

It ruffles wrists of posts,
As ankles of the queen, —
Then stills its artisans like ghosts,
Denying they have been.

EMILY DICKINSON

THE RAINBOW*

I saw the lovely arch
Of Rainbow span the sky,
The gold sun burning
As the rain swept by.

In bright-ringed solitude
The showery foliage shone
One lovely moment,
And the Bow was gone.

WALTER DE LA MARE

A FAREWELL

My fairest child, I have no song to give you;
  No lark could pipe to skies so dull and gray;
Yet, ere we part, one lesson I can leave you
  For every day.

Be good, sweet maid, and let who will be clever;
  Do noble things, not dream them, all day long:
And so make life, death, and that vast forever
  One grand, sweet song.

CHARLES KINGSLEY

ELDORADO

Gaily bedight
A gallant knight
In sunshine and in shadow,
Has journeyed long,
Singing a song,
In search of Eldorado.

But he grew old,
This knight so bold,
And o'er his heart a shadow
Fell as he found
No spot of ground
That looked like Eldorado.

* Reprinted by permission of The Literary Trustees of Walter de la Mare and the Society of Authors as their representative.

And, as his strength
Failed him at length,
He met a pilgrim shadow:
"Shadow," said he,
"Where can it be,
This land of Eldorado?"

"Over the mountains
Of the Moon,
Down the Valley of the Shadow,
Ride, boldly ride,"
The shade replied,
"If you seek for Eldorado!"

EDGAR ALLAN POE

FABLE

The mountain and the squirrel
Had a quarrel,
And the former called the latter "Little Prig";
Bun replied,
"You are doubtless very big;
But all sorts of things and weather
Must be taken in together,
To make up a year
And a sphere.
And I think it no disgrace
To occupy my place.
If I'm not so large as you,
You are not so small as I,
And not half so spry.
I'll not deny you make
A very pretty squirrel track.
Talents differ; all is well and wisely put;
If I cannot carry forests on my back,
Neither can you crack a nut."

RALPH WALDO EMERSON

MIRACLES

Why, who makes much of a miracle?
As to me I know of nothing else but miracles,
Whether I walk the streets of Manhattan,
Or dart my sight over the roofs of houses toward the sky,
Or wade with naked feet along the beach just in the edge of the water,
Or stand under trees in the woods . . .
Or watch honey-bees busy around the hive of a summer forenoon,
Or animals feeding in the fields,
Or birds, or the wonderfulness of insects in the air,
Or the wonderfulness of the sundown, or of the stars shining so quiet and bright,
Or the exquisite delicate thin curve of the new moon in spring;
These with the rest, one and all, are to me miracles,
The whole referring, yet each distinct and in its place.

To me every hour of the light and dark is a miracle,
Every cubic inch of space is a miracle,
Every square yard of the surface of the earth is spread with the same,
Every foot of the interior swarms with the same.

To me the sea is a continual miracle,
The fishes that swim — the rocks — the motion of the waves — the ships with men in them,
What stranger miracles are there?

WALT WHITMAN

From A PSALM OF LIFE

Lives of great men all remind us
We can make our lives sublime,
And, departing, leave behind us
Footprints in the sands of time; —

Footprints, that perhaps another,
Sailing o'er life's solemn main,
A forlorn and shipwrecked brother,
Seeing, shall take heart again.

Let us, then, be up and doing,
With a heart for any fate;
Still achieving, still pursuing,
Learn to labor and to wait.

HENRY WADSWORTH LONGFELLOW

INVICTUS

Out of the night that covers me,
Black as the pit from pole to pole,
I thank whatever gods may be
For my unconquerable soul.

In the fell clutch of circumstance
I have not winced nor cried aloud.
Under the bludgeonings of chance
My head is bloody, but unbowed.

Beyond this place of wrath and tears
Looms but the horror of the shade,
And yet the menace of the years
Finds, and shall find me, unafraid.

It matters not how strait the gate,
How charged with punishments the scroll,
I am the master of my fate:
I am the captain of my soul.

WILLIAM ERNEST HENLEY

◆◆◆

If I can stop one heart from breaking,
I shall not live in vain:
If I can ease one life the aching,
Or cool one pain,
Or help one fainting robin
Unto his nest again,
I shall not live in vain.

EMILY DICKINSON

OPPORTUNITY

Master of human destinies am I.
Fame, love, and fortune on my footsteps wait,
Cities and fields I walk; I penetrate
Deserts and seas remote, and, passing by
Hovel, and mart, and palace, soon or late
I knock unbidden, once at every gate!

If sleeping, wake — if feasting, rise before
I turn away. It is the hour of fate,
And they who follow me reach every state
Mortals desire, and conquer every foe
Save death; but those who doubt or hesitate,
Condemned to failure, penury and woe,
Seek me in vain and uselessly implore,
I answer not and I return no more.

John James Ingalls

BE LIKE THE BIRD

Be like the bird, who
Halting in his flight
On limb too slight
Feels it give way beneath him,
Yet sings
Knowing he hath wings.

Victor Hugo

THE PILGRIM

Who would true valour see,
Let him come hither!
One here will constant be,
Come wind, come weather;
There's no discouragement
Shall make him once relent
His firm-avowed intent
To be a Pilgrim.

Whoso beset him round
With dismal stories,
Do but themselves confound;
His strength the more is.
No lion can him fright;
He'll with a giant fight;
But he will have a right
To be a Pilgrim.

Nor enemy, nor friend,
Can daunt his spirit;
He knows he at the end
Shall Life inherit: —
Then, fancies, fly away;
He'll not fear what men say;
He'll labour, night and day,
To be a Pilgrim.

JOHN BUNYAN

◈◈◈

I'm nobody! Who are you?
Are you nobody too?
Then there's a pair of us — don't tell!
They'd banish us, you know.

How dreary to be somebody!
How public, like a frog
To tell your name the livelong day
To an admiring bog!

EMILY DICKINSON

DO YOU FEAR THE WIND?

Do you fear the force of the wind
The slash of the rain?
Go face them and fight them,
Be savage again.
Go hungry and cold like the wolf,
Go wade like the crane:

The palms of your hands will thicken,
The skin of your cheek will tan,
You'll grow ragged and weary and swarthy,
But you'll walk like a man!

HAMLIN GARLAND

THE WONDERFUL WORLD

Great, wide, beautiful, wonderful world,
With the wonderful water round you curled,
And the wonderful grass upon your breast,
World, you are beautifully dressed.

The wonderful air is over me,
And the wonderful wind is shaking the tree —
It walks on the water, and whirls the mills,
And talks to itself on the tops of the hills.

You friendly Earth! how far do you go,
With the wheat-fields that nod and the rivers that flow,
With cities and gardens and cliffs and isles,
And people upon you for thousands of miles?

Ah! you are so great, and I am so small,
I tremble to think of you, World, at all;
And yet, when I said my prayers to-day,
A whisper inside me seemed to say,
"You are more than the Earth, though you are such a dot:
You can love and think, and the Earth cannot!"

William Brighty Rands

I HEAR AMERICA SINGING

I hear America singing, the varied carols I hear;
Those of mechanics — each one singing his, as it should be, blithe and strong;
The carpenter singing his, as he measures his plank or beam,
The mason singing his, as he makes ready for work, or leaves off work;
The boatman singing what belongs to him in his boat — the deckhand singing on the steamboat deck;
The shoemaker singing as he sits on his bench — the hatter singing as he stands;
The woodcutter's song — the ploughboy's on his way in the morning, or at noon intermission, or at sundown;
The delicious singing of the mother — or of the young wife at work — or of the girl sewing or washing —
Each singing what belongs to him or her and to none else;
The day what belongs to the day — at night, the party of young fellows, robust, friendly,
Singing, with open mouths, their strong melodious songs.

Walt Whitman

AN EMERALD IS AS GREEN AS GRASS

An emerald is as green as grass;
A ruby red as blood;
A sapphire shines as blue as heaven;
A flint lies in the mud.

A diamond is a brilliant stone,
To catch the world's desire;
An opal holds a fiery spark;
But a flint holds fire.

CHRISTINA GEORGINA ROSSETTI

From THE VISION OF SIR LAUNFAL

And what is so rare as a day in June?
  Then, if ever, come perfect days;
Then Heaven tries earth if it be in tune,
  And over it softly her warm ear lays;
Whether we look, or whether we listen,
  We hear life murmur, or see it glisten;
Every clod feels a stir of might,
  An instinct within it that reaches and towers,
And, groping blindly above it for light,
  Climbs to a soul in grass and flowers.

JAMES RUSSELL LOWELL

◈◈◈

Will there really be a morning?
  Is there such a thing as day
Could I see it from the mountains
  If I were as tall as they?

Has it feet like water-lilies?
  Has it feathers like a bird?
Is it brought from famous countries
  Of which I have never heard?

Oh, some scholar! Oh, some sailor!
  Oh, some wise man from the skies!
Please to tell a little pilgrim
  Where the place called morning lies.

EMILY DICKINSON

AMERICA

My country 'tis of thee,
Sweet land of liberty,
   Of thee I sing;
Land where my fathers died,
Land of the Pilgrims' pride,
From every mountain-side
   Let Freedom ring.

My native country, thee,
Land of the noble free —
   Thy name I love;
I love thy rocks and rills,
Thy woods and templed hills;
My heart with rapture thrills
   Like that above.

Let music swell the breeze,
And ring from all the trees
   Sweet Freedom's song;
Let mortal tongues awake,
Let all that breath partake,
Let rocks their silence break —
   The sound prolong.

Our father's God to Thee,
Author of liberty,
   To Thee we sing;
Long may our land be bright
With Freedom's holy light;
Protect us by Thy might,
   Great God, our King.

SAMUEL FRANCIS SMITH

I STOOD TIPTOE UPON A LITTLE HILL

I stood tiptoe upon a little hill;
The air was cooling and so very still,
That the sweet buds which with a modest pride
Pull droopingly, in slanting curve aside,
Their scanty-leaved, and finely-tapering stems,
Had not yet lost their starry diadems
Caught from the early sobbing of the morn.

The clouds were pure and white as flocks new-shorn,
And fresh from the clear brook; sweetly they slept
On the blue fields of heaven, and then there crept
A little noiseless noise among the leaves,
For not the faintest motion could be seen
For not the faintest motion coul be seen
Of all the shades that slanted o'er the green.

JOHN KEATS

A NATION'S STRENGTH

Not gold, but only man can make
  A people great and strong;
Men who, for truth and honor's sake,
  Stand fast and suffer long.

Brave men who work while others sleep,
  Who dare while others fly —
They build a nation's pillars deep
  And lift them to the sky.

RALPH WALDO EMERSON

COLUMBUS*

Behind him lay the gray Azores,
  Behind the Gates of Hercules;
Before him not the ghost of shores,
  Before him only shoreless seas.
The good mate said: "Now must we pray,
  For lo! the very stars are gone.
Brave Admiral, speak, what shall I say?"
  "Why, say 'Sail on! sail on! and on!' "

"My men grow mutinous day by day;
  My men grow ghastly wan and weak."
The stout mate thought of home; a spray
  Of salt wave washed his swarthy cheek.
"What shall I say, brave Admiral, say,
  If we sight naught but seas at dawn?"
"Why, you shall say at break of day,
  'Sail on! sail on! sail on! and on!' "

* Reprinted by permission of Juanita Miller.

They sailed and sailed, as winds might blow,
  Until at last the blanched mate said,
"Why, now not even God would know
  Should I and all my men fall dead.
These very winds forget their way,
  For God from these dread seas is gone.
Now speak, brave Admiral, speak and say"—
  He said: "Sail on! Sail on! and on!"

They sailed. They sailed. Then spake the mate:
  "This mad sea shows his teeth tonight.
He curls his lip, he lies in wait,
  With lifted teeth, as if to bite!
Brave Admiral, say but one good word:
  What shall we do when hope is gone?"
The words leapt like a leaping sword:
  "Sail on! sail on! sail on! and on!"

Then, pale and worn, he kept his deck,
  And peered through darkness. Ah, that night
Of all dark nights! And then a speck —
  A light! a light! a light! a light!
It grew, a starlit flag unfurled!
  It grew to be Time's burst of dawn.
He gained a world; he gave that world
  Its grandest lesson: "On! sail on!"

JOAQUIN MILLER

THE THROSTLE

"Summer is coming, summer is coming,
  I know it, I know it, I know it.
Light again, leaf again, life again, love again,"
  Yes, my wild little Poet.

Sing the new year in under the blue.
  Last year you sang it as gladly.
"New, new, new, new!" Is it then so new
  That you should carol so madly?

"Love again, song again, nest again, young again,"
  Never a prophet so crazy!
And hardly a daisy as yet, little friend,
  See, there is hardly a daisy.

"Here again, here, here, here, happy year!"
O warble unchidden, unbidden!
Summer is coming, is coming, my dear,
And all the winters are hidden.

ALFRED TENNYSON

BE USEFUL

Be useful where thou livest, that they may
Both want and wish thy pleasing presence still.
— Find out men's wants and will,
And meet them there. All worldly joys go less
To the one joy of doing kindnesses.

GEORGE HERBERT

NOVEMBER FRIDAY*

(On the assassination of John Fitzgerald Kennedy)

This was the day an eagle died,
Torn from a topmost mountain crag:
Three times the thunder crashed,
Shattering the light.

Sullen wind on the mountain drummed;
Sudden lightning seared the earth;
Night plunged like a black-winged bird,
Shutting out the sun.

WILLIAM E. CARROLL

I HEARD A BIRD SING

I heard a bird sing,
In the dark of December
A magical thing
And sweet to remember.

"We are nearer to Spring
Than we were in September,"
I heard a bird sing
In the dark of December.

OLIVER HERFORD

* With the permission of the author, an English teacher in the Pittsburgh Public Schools.

. . . Much time has passed since the first colonists came to rocky shores and dark forests of an unknown continent, much time since President Washington led a young people into the experience of nationhood, much time since President Lincoln saw the American nation through the ordeal of fraternal war — and in these years our population, our plenty and our power have all grown apace. Today we are a nation of nearly two hundred million souls, stretching from coast to coast, on into the Pacific and North toward the Arctic, a nation enjoying the fruits of an ever-expanding agriculture and industry and achieving standards of living unknown in previous history. We give our humble thanks for this.

Yet, as our power has grown, so has our peril. Today we give our thanks, most of all, for the ideals of honor and faith we inherit from our forefathers — for the decency of purpose, steadfastness of resolve and strength of will, for the courage and the humility, which they possessed and which we must seek every day to emulate. As we express our gratitude, we must never forget that the highest appreciation is not to utter words but to live by them.

Let us therefore proclaim our gratitude to Providence for manifold blessings — let us be humbly thankful for inherited ideals — and let us resolve to share those blessings and those ideals with our fellow human beings throughout the world . . .

John Fitzgerald Kennedy

THE SNARE*

I hear a sudden cry of pain!
There is a rabbit in a snare;
Now I hear the cry again,
But I cannot tell from where.

But I cannot tell from where.
He is calling out for aid!
Crying on the frightened air,
Making everything afraid!

* Reprinted with permission of The Macmillan Company from *Collected Poems* by James Stephens. Copyright 1915 by The Macmillan Company, renewed 1943 by James Stephens.

Making everything afraid!
Wrinkling up his little face!
As he cries again for aid;
— And I cannot find the place!

And I cannot find the place
Where his paw is in the snare!
Little One! Oh, Little One!
I am searching everywhere!

JAMES STEPHENS

SWIFT THINGS ARE BEAUTIFUL*

Swift things are beautiful:
Swallows and deer,
And lightning that falls
Bright-veined and clear,
Rivers and meteors,
Wind in the wheat,
The strong-withered horse,
The runner's sure feet.

And slow things are beautiful:
The closing of day,
The pause of the wave
That curves downward to spray,
The ember that crumbles,
The opening flower,
And the ox that moves on
In the quiet of power.

ELIZABETH COATSWORTH

THE DAY WILL BRING SOME LOVELY THING†

"The day will bring some lovely thing,"
I say it over each new dawn:
"Some gay, adventurous thing to hold
Against my heart when it is gone."
And so I rise and go to meet

* Reprinted with permission of The Macmillan Company from *Away Goes Sally* by Elizabeth Coatsworth. Copyright 1934 by The Macmillan Company, renewed 1962 by Elizabeth Coatsworth Beston.

† From *The Poems of Inspiration and Courage,* Grace Noll Crowell © 1965 Grace Noll Crowell, Harper & Row, Publishers Inc.

I come upon it unaware —
Some sudden beauty without name:
A snatch of song — a breath of pine —
A poem lit with golden flame;
High tangled bird notes — keenly thinned —
Like flying color on the wind.

No day has ever failed me quite —
Before the grayest day is done,
I come upon some misty bloom
Or a late line of crimson sun.
Each night I pause — remembering
Some gay, adventurous, lovely thing.

GRACE NOLL CROWELL

THE BOY SCOUT OATH*

On my honor I will do my best —
To do my duty to God and my country, and to obey the Scout Law;
To help other people at all times;
To keep myself physically strong, mentally awake, and morally straight.

BOY SCOUTS OF AMERICA

THE GIRL SCOUT PROMISE†

On my honor, I will try:
To do my duty to God and my country,
To help other people at all times,
To obey the Girl Scout Laws.

GIRL SCOUTS OF THE
UNITED STATES OF AMERICA

◈◈◈

The morns are meeker than they were,
The nuts are getting brown;
The berry's cheek is plumper,
The rose is out of town.

* Reprinted by permission of the Boy Scouts of America National Council.
† Used by permission of the Girl Scouts of the U.S.A.

The maple wears a gayer scarf,
The field a scarlet gown.
Lest I should be old-fashioned,
I'll put a trinket on.

EMILY DICKINSON

A SMILE

Let others cheer the winning man,
There's one I hold worth while;
'Tis he who does the best he can,
Then loses with a smile.
Beaten he is, but not to stay
Down with the rank and file;
That man will win some other day,
Who loses with a smile.

ANONYMOUS

ENGLISH*

As gardens grow with flowers,
English grows with words,
Words that have secret powers,
Words that give joy like birds.

Some of the words you say,
Both in and out of school,
Are brighter than the day,
And deeper than a pool.

Some words there are that dance,
Some words there are that sigh,
The fool's words come by chance,
The poet's to heaven fly.

When you are grown, your tongue
Should give the joy of birds,
Get while you are young
The gift of English words.

ELEANOR FARJEON

* *English* from *Poems for Children* by Eleanor Farjeon. Copyright 1938 by Eleanor Farjeon. Published by J. B. Lippincott Company.

REFLECTION*

Beauty is a lily,
Sparkling and cool,
Its bowl of dewy petals
Stemming in a pool.

Meditate on beauty,
Hold it, and look! —
Beauty shall be doubled, —
A lily in a brook.

LEW SARETT

From THE AMERICAN FLAG

When Freedom, from her mountain height,
Unfurled her standard to the air,
She tore the azure robe of night,
And set the stars of glory there;
She mingled with its gorgeous dyes
The milky baldric of the skies,
And striped its pure, celestial white
With streakings of the morning light;
Then, from his mansion in the sun,
She called her eagle bearer down,
And gave into his mighty hand
The symbol of her chosen land.

JOSEPH RODMAN DRAKE

THE MAGIC PIPER†

There piped a piper in the wood
  Strange music — soft and sweet —
And all the little wild things
  Came hurrying to his feet.

They sat around him on the grass,
  Enchanted, unafraid,
And listened, as with shining eyes
  Sweet melodies he made.

---

* From *Wings Against the Moon* by Lew Sarett. Copyright 1931 by Henry Holt and Company, Inc., 1959 by Alma Johnson Sarett. Reprinted with permission of Mrs. Sarett.

† From *Book of a Thousand Poems,* reprinted by permission of Evans Brothers Limited, London.

The wood grew green, and flowers sprang up,
The birds began to sing;
For the music it was magic,
And the piper's name was — Spring!

E. L. Marsh

◈◈◈

Let us then stand by the constitution as it is, and by our country as it is, one, united, and entire; let it be a truth engraven on our hearts; let it be borne on the flag under which we rally in every exigency, that we have one country, one constitution, one destiny.

Daniel Webster
Speech, New York, March 15, 1837

SONG

Piping down the valleys wild,
Piping songs of pleasant glee,
On a cloud I saw a child,
And he laughing said to me:

"Pipe a song about a lamb!"
So I piped with merry cheer.
"Piper, pipe that song again";
So I piped: he wept to hear.

"Drop thy pipe, thy happy pipe;
Sing thy songs of happy cheer!"
So I sang the same again,
While he wept with joy to hear.

"Piper, sit thee down and write
In a book that all may read."
So he vanished from my sight;
And I plucked a hollow reed,

And I made a rural pen,
And I stained the water clear,
And I wrote my happy songs
Every child may joy to hear.

William Blake

SCHOOL CREED

This is our school,
Let peace dwell here,
Let the room be full of contentment,
Let love abide here.
Love of one another,
Love of mankind,
Love of life itself,
And love of God.
Let us remember
That as many hands build a house
So many hearts make a school.

FROM A SCHOOL IN CANADA

PERSEVERE

The fisher who draws in his net too soon,
  Won't have any fish to sell;
The child who shuts up his book too soon,
  Won't learn any lessons well.

If you would have your learning stay,
  Be patient — don't learn too fast;
The man who travels a mile each day,
  May get round the world at last.

ANONYMOUS

From RAIN IN SUMMER

How beautiful is the rain!
After the dust and heat,
In the broad and fiery street,
In the narrow lane,
How beautiful is the rain!

How it clatters along the roofs,
Like the tramp of hoofs!
How it gushes and struggles out
From the throat of the overflowing spout!

Across the window pane
It pours and pours;
And swift and wide,
With a muddy tide,
Like a river down the gutter roars
The rain, the welcome rain!

HENRY WADSWORTH LONGFELLOW

INAUGURAL ADDRESS

. . . In the long history of the world, only a few generations have been granted the role of defending freedom in its hour of maximum danger. I do not shrink from this responsibility — I welcome it. I do not believe that any of us would exchange places with any other people or any other generation. The energy, the faith and the devotion which we bring to this endeavor will light our country and all who serve it — and the glow from that fire can truly light the world.

And so, my fellow Americans: ask not what your country can do for you — ask what you can do for your country . . .

JOHN FITZGERALD KENNEDY

RULES FOR THE ROAD*

Stand straight:
Step firmly, throw your weight:
The heaven is high above your head,
The good gray road is faithful to your tread.

Be strong:
Sing to your heart a battle song:
Though hidden foemen lie in wait,
Something is in you that can smile at Fate.

Press through:
Nothing can harm you if you are true.
And when night comes, rest:
The earth is friendly as a mother's breast.

EDWIN MARKHAM

* From *Gates of Paradise and Other Poems* by Edwin Markham. Reprinted by permission of Virgil Markham.

LEND A HAND

Lend a hand to one another
In the daily toil of life;
When we meet a weaker brother,
Let us help him in the strife.
There is none so rich but may,
In his turn, be forced to borrow;
And the poor man's lot today
May become our own tomorrow.

ANONYMOUS

SUN AND WIND*

The old sun, the gold sun,
With lovely May returning,
Went among the chestnut trees
And set their candles burning.

The cold winds, the bold winds,
Came down like Goths and Vandals,
And went among the chestnut trees
Blowing out their candles.

ELEANOR FARJEON

THE TWENTY-SECOND OF FEBRUARY

Pale is the February sky,
And brief the mid-day's sunny hours;
The wind-swept forest seems to sigh
For the sweet time of leaves and flowers.

Yet has no month a prouder day,
Not even when the summer broods
O'er meadows in their fresh array,
Or autumn tints the glowing woods.

For this chill season now again
Brings, in its annual round, the morn
When, greatest of the sons of men,
Our glorious Washington was born.

Lo, where, beneath an icy shield,
   Calmly the mighty Hudson flows!
By snow-clad fell and frozen field,
   Broadening the lordly river goes.

The wildest storm that sweeps through space,
   And rends the oak with sudden force,
Can raise no ripple on his face,
   Or slacken his majestic course.

Thus, 'mid the wreck of thrones, shall live
   Unmarred, undimmed, our hero's fame,
And years succeeding years shall give
   Increase of honors to his name.

WILLIAM CULLEN BRYANT

◈◈◈

Dear March, come in!
How glad I am!
I looked for you before.
Put down your hat —
You must have walked —
How out of breath you are!
Dear March, how are you?
And the rest?
Did you leave Nature well?
Oh, March, come right upstairs with me,
I have so much to tell!
Who knocks? That April!
Lock the door!
I will not be pursued!
He stayed away a year, to call
When I am occupied.

EMILY DICKINSON

OCTOBER'S BRIGHT BLUE WEATHER

O suns and skies and clouds of June,
   And flowers of June together,
Ye cannot rival for one hour
   October's bright blue weather;

When loud the bumblebee makes haste,
   Belated, thriftless vagrant,
And goldenrod is dying fast,
   And lanes with grapes are fragrant;

When gentians roll their fringes tight
  To save them for the morning,
And chestnuts fall from satin burrs
  Without a sound of warning;

When on the ground red apples lie
  In piles like jewels shining,
And redder still on old stone walls
  Are leaves of woodbine twining;

When all the lovely wayside things
  Their white-winged seeds are sowing,
And in the fields, still green and fair,
  Late aftermaths are growing;

When springs run low, and on the brooks,
  In idle golden freighting,
Bright leaves sink noiseless in the hush
  Of woods, for winter waiting;

When comrades seek sweet country haunts,
  By twos and twos together,
And count like misers, hour by hour,
  October's bright blue weather.

O sun and skies and flowers of June,
  Count all your boasts together,
Love loveth best of all the year
  October's bright blue weather.

HELEN HUNT JACKSON

THANKSGIVING DAY

Over the river and through the wood,
  To grandfather's house we go;
    The horse knows the way
    To carry the sleigh
  Through the white and drifted snow.

Over the river and through the wood —
  Oh, how the wind does blow!
    It stings the toes
    And bites the nose,
  As over the ground we go.

Over the river and through the wood,
  To have a first-rate play.
    Hear the bells ring,
    "Ting-a-ling-ding!"
  Hurrah for Thanksgiving Day!

Over the river and through the wood
  Trot fast, my dapple-gray!
    Spring over the ground,
    Like a hunting-hound!
  For this is Thanksgiving Day.

Over the river and through the wood —
  And straight through the barnyard gate.
    We seem to go
    Extremely slow, —
  It is so hard to wait!

Over the river and through the wood —
  Now grandmother's cap I spy!
    Hurrah for the fun!
    Is the pudding done?
  Hurrah for the pumpkin-pie!

LYDIA MARIA CHILD

THE MOUSE THAT GNAWED THE OAK-TREE DOWN*

The mouse that gnawed the oak-tree down
Began his task in early life.
He kept so busy with his teeth
He had no time to take a wife.

He gnawed and gnawed through sun and rain
When the ambitious fit was on,
Then rested in the sawdust till
A month of idleness had gone.

He did not move about to hunt
The coteries of mousie-men.
He was a snail-paced, stupid thing
Until he cared to gnaw again.

* Reprinted with permission of The Macmillan Company from *The Congo and Other Poems* by Vachel Lindsay. Copyright 1914 by The Macmillan Company, renewed 1942 by Elizabeth C. Lindsay.

The mouse that gnawed the oak-tree down,
When that tough foe was at his feet —
Found in the stump no angel-cake
Nor buttered bread, nor cheese, nor meat —

The forest-roof let in the sky.
"This light is worth the work," said he.
"I'll make this ancient swamp more light!"
And started on another tree.

VACHEL LINDSAY

WORTH WHILE*

It is easy enough to be pleasant,
When life flows by like a song,
But the man worth while is one who will smile,
When everything goes dead wrong.
For the test of the heart is trouble,
And it always comes with the years,
And the smile that is worth the praises of earth
Is the one that shines through tears.

ELLA WHEELER WILCOX

THE RIVALS†

I heard a bird at dawn
Singing sweetly on a tree,
That the dew was on the lawn,
And the wind was on the lea;
But I didn't listen to him,
For he didn't sing to me.

I didn't listen to him,
For he didn't sing to me
That the dew was on the lawn
And the wind was on the lea!
I was singing at the time,
Just as prettily as he!

* From *Poems of Sentiment* by Ella Wheeler Wilcox. Used by permission of Rand McNally and Company.

† Reprinted with permission of The Macmillan Company from *Collected Poems* by James Stephens. Copyright 1915 by The Macmillan Company, renewed 1943 by James Stephens.

I was singing all the time,
Just as prettily as he,
About the dew upon the lawn,
And the wind upon the lea!
So I didn't listen to him
As he sang upon a tree!

JAMES STEPHENS

HOW GRAY THE RAIN*

How gray the rain
And gray the world
And gray the rain clouds overhead,
When suddenly
Some cloud is furled
And there is gleaming sun instead!

The raindrops drip
Prismatic light,
And trees and meadows burn in green,
And arched in air
Serene and bright
The rainbow all at once is seen.

Serene and bright
The rainbow stands
That was not anywhere before,
And so may joy
Fill empty hands
When someone enters through a door.

ELIZABETH COATSWORTH

ROADS†

A road might lead to anywhere —
To harbor towns and quays,
Or to a witch's pointed house
Hidden by bristly trees.

It might lead past the tailor's door,
  Where he sews with needle and thread,
Or by Miss Pim the milliner's,
  With her hats for every head.
It might be a road to a great, dark cave
  With treasure and gold piled high,
Or a road with a mountain tied to its end,
  Blue-humped against the sky.
Oh, a road might lead you anywhere —
  To Mexico or Maine.
But then, it might just fool you, and —
  Lead you back home again!

RACHEL FIELD

FRINGED GENTIANS*

Near where I live there is a lake
As blue as blue can be; winds make
It dance as they go blowing by.
I think it curtsies to the sky.

It's just a lake of lovely flowers,
And my Mamma says they are ours;
But they are not like those we grow
To be our very own, you know.

We have a splendid garden, there
Are lots of flowers everywhere;
Roses, and pinks, and four-o'clocks,
And hollyhocks, and evening stocks.

Mamma lets us pick them, but never
Must we pick any gentians — ever!
For if we carried them away
They'd die of homesickness that day.

AMY LOWELL

* From *A Dome of Many-coloured Glass* by Amy Lowell. Reprinted by permission of Houghton Mifflin Company.

FOUR-LEAF CLOVER

I know a place where the sun is like gold,
  And the cherry blooms burst with snow,
And down underneath is the loveliest nook,
  Where the four-leaf clovers grow.

One leaf is for hope, and one is for faith,
  And one is for love, you know,
And God put another one in for luck —
  If you search, you will find where they grow.

But you must have hope, and you must have faith,
  You must love and be strong — and so
If you work, if you wait, you will find the place
  Where the four-leaf clovers grow.

Ella Higginson

RING AROUND THE WORLD*

Ring around the world
Taking hands together
All across the temperate
And the torrid weather.
Past the royal palm-trees
By the ocean sand
Make a ring around the world
Taking each other's hand;
In the valleys, on the hill,
Over the prairie spaces,
There's a ring around the world
Made of children's friendly faces.

Annette Wynne

* *Ring Around the World* from *All Through the Year* by Annette Wynne. Copyright 1932, 1960 by Annette Wynne. Reprinted by permission of J. B. Lippincott Company.

VELVET SHOES*

Let us walk in the white snow
In a soundless space;
With footsteps quiet and slow,
At a tranquil pace,
Under veils of white lace.

I shall go shod in silk,
And you in wool,
White as a white cow's milk,
More beautiful
Than the breast of a gull.

We shall walk through the still town
In a windless peace;
We shall step upon white down,
Upon silver fleece,
Upon softer than these.

We shall walk in velvet shoes;
Wherever we go
Silence will fall like dews
On white silence below.
We shall walk in the snow.

ELINOR WYLIE

GROUND HOG DAY†

In February when few gusty flakes
Above the frozen sheets of snow still hover,
Out of his hole the sleepy ground hog breaks
To peek around and see if winter's over.

Now if he find his shadow, back he shies
To nap while deeper drifts the wind shall bring;
But if no shadow shows beneath dark skies
He waddles through the ditch to look for spring.

MARNIE POMEROY

THE PHILOSOPHY OF PRESIDENT LYNDON B. JOHNSON

Reprinted from *U. S. News & World Report,* December 2, 1963, published at Washington, D.C.

. . . I am a great believer in the philosophy of the prophet Isaiah, "Come now, and let us reason together."

. . . Hitler didn't have to reason with people; he could march them. But our system is a Government of reason, or judgment, where men have dignity and where each can express himself.

The Supreme Court can pass on what the Congress does, and the President can pass on what the Congress does, and the Congress can pass on what both of them do. It's three separate, independent branches of Government — each with respect for each other. And it has resulted in our having a Government with the maximum freedom. Sometimes it is a little tardy. We have some delays. It's expensive, and we have some inefficiency. But it works, and we have freedom and the highest standard of living the world has ever known — far higher than in the supposedly efficient dictatorships . . .*

SONG OF THE SETTLERS†

Freedom is a hard-bought thing —
A gift no man can give.
For some, a way of dying,
For most, a way to live.

---

† From *A Mirror for the Sky* by Jessamyn West. Reprinted by permission of Jessamyn West. Copyright © 1946, 1948 by Jessamyn West.

Freedom is a hard-bought thing —
A rifle in the hand,
The horses hitched at sunup,
A harvest in the land.

Freedom is a hard-bought thing —
A massacre, a bloody rout,
The candles lit at nightfall,
And the night shut out.

Freedom is a hard-bought thing —
An arrow in the back,
The wind in the long corn rows,
And the hay in the rack.

Freedom is a way of living,
A song, a mighty cry.
Freedom is the bread we eat.
Let it be the way we die.

JESSAMYN WEST

◈◈◈

Sink or swin, live or die, survive or perish, I give my hand and my heart to this vote . . . Sir, I know the uncertainty of human affairs, but I see, I see clearly, through this day's business. You and I, indeed, may rue it. We may not live to see the time when this Declaration shall be made good . . . But whatever may be our fate, be assured, be assured, that this Declaration will stand . . .

Sir, before God, I believe the hour is come. My judgment approves this measure, and my whole heart is in it. All that I have, and all that I am, and all that I hope in this life, I am now ready here to stake upon it; and I leave off as I began, that live or die, survive or perish, I am for the Declaration. It is my living sentiment, and by the blessing of God it shall be my dying sentiment: independence, now and INDEPENDENCE FOREVER.

Speech attributed to JOHN ADAMS, *by Daniel Webster in a eulogy on Adams, delivered August 2, 1826.*

THE MIST AND I*

I like the fall,
The mist and all.
I like the night owl's
Lonely call —
And wailing sound
Of wind around.

I like the gray
November day,
And bare, dead boughs
That coldly sway
Against my pane.
I like the rain.

I like to sit
And laugh at it —
And tend
My cozy fire a bit.
I like the fall —
The mist and all.

DIXIE WILLSON

WHITE FIELDS†

In winter-time we go
Walking in the fields of snow
Where there is no grass at all;
Where the top of every wall,
Every fence, and every tree,
Is a white as white can be.

Pointing out the way we came —
Every one of them the same —
All across the fields there be
Prints in silver filigree;
And our mothers always know,
By the footprints in the snow,
Where it is the children go.

JAMES STEPHENS

* Title changed at author's request. From *Child Life Magazine,* copyright 1924, 1952 by Rand McNally and Company. Reprinted by permission of Rand McNally and Company and Dixie Willson.

† Reprinted with permission of The Macmillan Company from *Collected Poems* by James Stephens. Copyright 1915 by The Macmillan Company, renewed 1943 by James Stephens.

From SANTA FILOMENA

Whene'er a noble deed is wrought,
Whene'er is spoken a noble thought,
  Our hearts, in glad surprise,
  To higher levels rise.

Honor to those whose words or deeds
Thus help us in our daily needs,
  And by their overflow
  Raise us from what is low!

HENRY WADSWORTH LONGFELLOW

THE WARM OF HEART*

The warm of heart shall never lack a fire
However far he roam.
Although he live forever among strangers
He cannot lack a home.

For strangers are not strangers to his spirit,
And each house seems his own,
And by the fire of his loving-kindness
He cannot sit alone.

ELIZABETH COATSWORTH

SOLIDARITY†

(Translated from the Spanish by Mildred E. Johnson)

Little lark, let us sing a song!
Waterfall, let us leap along!
Rivulet, let us run with mirth!
Diamond, let us be very bright!
Eagle, now let us take our flight!
Dawn of day, let us have new birth!
    Sing a song!
    Leap along!

---

* Reprinted with permission of The Macmillan Company from *Five Bushel Farm* by Elizabeth Coatsworth. Copyright 1939 by The Macmillan Company.

† *Swan, Cygnets, and Owl; An Anthology of Modernist Poetry in Spanish America*, Mildred E. Johnson, translator. University of Missouri Studies XXIX. Columbia, University of Missouri Press, 1956.

Run with mirth!
Be very bright!
Take our flight!
Have new birth!

AMADO NERVO

THE MAN WITHOUT A COUNTRY*

In a famous short story called *The Man Without a Country*, the chief character, Philip Nolan, an officer in the Army of the United States, cursed his country in a moment of anger and was sentenced to spend the rest of his life on a ship. At one point in the story, he expressed his deep regret over all that he had lost in these words to a midshipman:

> "And for your country, boy" . . . "and for that flag" . . . "never dream a dream but of serving her as she bids you, though the service carry you through a thousand hells. No matter what happens to you, no matter who flatters you or who abuses you, never look at another flag, never let a night pass but you pray God to bless that flag. Remember, boy, that behind all these men you have to do with, behind officers, and government, and people even, there is the Country Herself, your Country, and that you belong to Her as you belong to your own mother. Stand by Her, boy, as you would stand by your mother . . ,"

EDWARD EVERETT HALE

. . . If I were to choose the sights, the sounds, the fragrances I most would want to see and hear and smell — among all the delights of the open world — on a final day on earth, I think I would choose these: the clear, ethereal song of a white-throated sparrow singing at dawn; the smell of pine trees in the heat of noon; the lonely calling of Canada geese; the sight of a dragonfly glinting in the sunshine; the voice of a hermit thrush far in a darkening woods at evening; and — most spiritual and moving of sights — the white cathedral of a cumulus cloud floating serenely in the blue of the sky.†

EDWIN WAY TEALE

* From *The Man Without a Country* by Edward Everett Hale. Copyright 1951 by Houghton Mifflin Company and reprinted with permission. Originally published 1899.

† From *The Lost Woods* by Edwin Way Teale. Copyright 1945 by Edwin Way Teale. Reprinted by permission of Dodd, Mead and Company.

POETRY AND PROSE

Grades 7–9

LATIMER SCHOOL CODE AND SLOGAN

I would be Loyal, for the honor of the school is mine.
I would be Ambitious, for ambition is the foundation of progress.
I would be Trustworthy, for people have faith in me.
I would be Industrious, for what I am to be I am now becoming.
I would be Merry, for smiles are contagious.
I would be Enthusiastic, for spirit makes us win.
I would be Ready to serve at a moment's notice.

DO IT BECAUSE IT IS RIGHT!

FOUR THINGS

Four things a man must learn to do
If he would make his record true:
To think without confusion clearly;
To love his fellow men sincerely;
To act from honest motives purely;
To trust in God and heaven securely.

HENRY VAN DYKE

From HAMLET

There, — my blessing with you!
And these few precepts in thy memory
See thou character. Give thy thoughts no tongue,
Nor any unproportion'd thought his act.
Be thou familiar, but by no means vulgar.
The friends thou hast, and their adoption tried,
Grapple them to thy soul with hoops of steel;
But do not dull thy palm with entertainment
Of each new-hatch'd, unfledg'd comrade. Beware
Of entrance to a quarrel; but, being in,
Bear't that the opposed may beware of thee.
Give every man thine ear, but few thy voice:
Take each man's censure, but reserve thy judgment.
Costly thy habit as thy purse can buy,
But not expressed in fancy; rich, not gaudy:
For the apparel oft proclaims the man.

. . . .

Neither a borrower nor a lender be,
For a loan oft loses both itself and friend,
And borrowing dulls the edge of husbandry.
This above all, — to thine own self be true;
And it must follow, as the night the day,
Thou canst not then be false to any man.

WILLIAM SHAKESPEARE

From NATURE

It seems as if the day was not wholly profane in which we have given heed to some natural object. The fall of snowflakes in a still air, preserving to each crystal its perfect form; the blowing of sleet over a wide sheet of water, and over plains; the waving rye field; the mimic waving of acres of houstonia, whose innumerable florets whiten and ripple before the eye; the reflection of trees and flowers in glassy lakes; the musical steaming odorous south wind, which converts all trees to wind harps; the crackling and spurting of hemlock in the flames; or of pine logs, which yield glory to the walls and faces in the sitting room — these are the music and pictures of the most ancient religion.

RALPH WALDO EMERSON

GOALS FOR TOMORROW

The hope of our free society lies in the public schools. It is here that the society of tomorrow begins to take shape; here that the SPARK, the STRENGTH, and the CHARACTER of our democracy are generated.

The words SPARK, STRENGTH, and CHARACTER might also be used to describe what should happen within each child as he goes through school.

Those three words sum up the goals of education. The school should help each child, whatever his differing abilities and attitudes, strike the SPARK that will ignite his imagination so that he will want to realize his potential. There should be a common core of knowledge, values, and basic skills available to all.

Every child should get from his education the STRENGTH to face his life's work and responsibilities. He must learn to think rationally and critically so that education can become a lifelong process.

The development of CHARACTER must be an ever-present goal of all phases of education, curricular and extracurricular.

Tomorrow's schools will provide the SPARK, the STRENGTH, and the CHARACTER that the United States has received from them in the past . . . that this generation so desperately needs today.

CARSTEN AHRENS

◈◈◈

The last letter received by President Andrew Jackson from his mother:

Andrew, if I should not see you again I wish you to remember some things I have already said to you: In this world you will have to make your own way. To do that you must have friends. You can make friends by being honest, and you can keep them by being steadfast. You must keep in mind that friends worth having will in the long run expect as much from you as they give to you. To forget an obligation or be ungrateful for a kindness is a base crime — not merely a fault or a sin but an actual crime. Men guilty of it sooner or later must suffer the penalty. In personal conduct be always polite, but never obsequious. No one will respect you more than you esteem yourself. Avoid quarrels as long as you can without yielding to imposition. But sustain your manhood always. Never bring a suit of law for assault and battery or for defamation. The law affords no remedy for such outrages that can satisfy the feelings of a true man. Never wound the feelings of others. Never brook wanton outrage upon your own feelings. If ever you have to vindicate your feelings or defend your honor do it calmly. If angry at first, wait till your wrath cools before you proceed.

From SONG OF MYSELF

I believe a leaf of grass is no less than the
  journeywork of the stars,
And the pismire is equally perfect, and a grain
  of sand, and the egg of the wren,
And the tree toad is a chef-d'oeuvre for the highest,
And the running blackberry would adorn the
  parlors of heaven,
And the narrowest hinge in my hand puts to
  scorn all machinery,
And the cow crunching with depress'd head
  surpasses any statue,
And a mouse is miracle enough to stagger
  sextillions of infidels.

WALT WHITMAN

Finish every day and be done with it. You have done what you could. Some blunders and absurdities no doubt crept in; forget them as soon as you can. Tomorrow is a new day; begin it well and serenely and with too high a spirit to be cumbered with your old nonsense. This day is all that is good and fair. It is too dear, with its hopes and invitations, to waste a moment on the yesterdays.

RALPH WALDO EMERSON

From A MAN'S A MAN FOR A' THAT

Then let us pray that come it may
(As come it will for a' that)
That sense and worth o'er all the earth
Shall bear the gree an' a' that!
For a' that, an' a' that,
It's comin' yet for a' that
That man to man the world o'er
Shall brothers be for a' that!

ROBERT BURNS

◈◈◈

There is no frigate like a book
To take us lands away,
Nor any courser like a page
Of prancing poetry.

This traverse may the poorest take
Without oppress of toll;
How frugal is the chariot
That bears a human soul!

EMILY DICKINSON

◈◈◈

He ate and drank the precious words,
His spirit grew robust;
He knew no more that he was poor,
Nor that his frame was dust.

He danced along the dingy days,
And this bequest of wings
Was but a book. What liberty
A loosened spirit brings.

EMILY DICKINSON

GOD, GIVE US MEN!

God, give us men! A time like this demands
Strong minds, great hearts, true faith and
  ready hands;
Men whom the lust of office does not kill;
Men whom the spoils of office cannot buy;
Men who possess opinions and a will;
Men who have honor; men who will not lie;
Men who can stand before a demagogue
And damn his treacherous flatteries without winking!
Tall men, sun-crowned, who live above the fog
In public duty and in private thinking;
For while the rabble, with their thumb-worn creeds,
Their large professions and their little deeds,
Mingle in selfish strife, lo! Freedom weeps,
Wrong rules the land and waiting Justice sleeps.

JOSIAH GILBERT HOLLAND

◈◈◈

I never saw a moor,
I never saw the sea;
Yet know I how the heather looks,
And what a wave must be.

I never spoke with God,
Nor visited in heaven.
Yet certain am I of the spot
As if the chart were given.

EMILY DICKINSON

◈◈◈

We never know how high we are
Till we are called to rise;
And then, if we are true to plan,
Our statures touch the skies.

The heroisms we recite
Would be a daily thing,
Did not ourselves the cubits warp
For fear to be a king.

EMILY DICKINSON

Words are instruments of music; an ignorant man uses them for jargon; but when a master touches them they have unexpected life and soul. Some words sound out like drums; some breathe memories sweet as flutes; some call like a clarionet; some show a charge like trumpets; some are sweet as children's talk; others rich as a mother's answering back.

ANONYMOUS

THE CELESTIAL SURGEON

If I have faltered more or less
In my great task of happiness;
If I have moved among my race
And shown no glorious morning face;
If beams from happy human eyes
Have moved me not; if morning skies,
Books, and my food, and summer rain
Knocked on my sullen heart in vain: —
Lord, thy most pointed pleasure take,
And stab my spirit broad awake;
Or, Lord, if too obdurate I,
Choose thou, before that spirit die,
A piercing pain, a killing sin,
And to my dead heart run them in!

ROBERT LOUIS STEVENSON

ABOU BEN ADHEM

Abou Ben Adhem (may his tribe increase!)
Awoke one night from a deep dream of peace,
And saw within the moonlight in his room,
Making it rich and like a lily in bloom,
An angel writing in a book of gold:
Exceeding peace had made Ben Adhem bold,
And to the presence in the room he said,
"What writes thou?" The vision raised its head,
And, with a look made of all sweet accord,
Answered, "The names of those who love the Lord."
"And is mine one?" said Abou. "Nay, not so,"
Replied the angel. Abou spoke more low,
But cheerly still; and said, "I pray thee, then,
Write me as one that loves his fellow-men."

The angel wrote, and vanished. The next night
It came again, with a great wakening light,

And showed the names whom love of God had blessed, —
And, lo! Ben Adhem's name led all the rest!

LEIGH HUNT

From "MEDITATION 17," DEVOTIONS UPON EMERGENT OCCASIONS

Who casts not up his eye to the sun when it rises? . . . Who bends not his ear to any bell, which upon any occasion rings? but who can remove it from that bell, which is passing a piece of himself out of this world? No man is an island, entire of itself; every man is a piece of the continent, a part of the main; if a clod be washed away by the sea, Europe is the less, as well as if a promontory were, as well as if a manor of thy friend's or of thine own were; any man's death diminishes me, because I am involved in mankind; And therefore never send to know for whom the bell tolls; It tolls for thee.

JOHN DONNE

MY HEART LEAPS UP

My heart leaps up when I behold
  A rainbow in the sky:
So was it when my life began;
So is it now I am a man;
So be it when I shall grow old,
  Or let me die!
The Child is father of the Man;
And I could wish my days to be
Bound each to each by natural piety.

WILLIAM WORDSWORTH

TOMORROW

Tomorrow's fate, though thou be wise,
Thou canst not tell nor yet surmise;
Pass, therefore, not today in vain,
For it will never come again.

OMAR KHAYYÁM

THE EAGLE

He clasps the crag with crooked hands;
Close to the sun in lonely lands,
Ringed with the azure world, he stands.
The wrinkled sea beneath him crawls;
He watches from his mountain walls,
And like a thunderbolt he falls.

ALFRED TENNYSON

INAUGURAL ADDRESS

. . . Since this country was founded, each generation of Americans has been summoned to give testimony to its national loyalty. The graves of young Americans who answered that call encircle the globe.

Now the trumpet summons us again — not as a call to bear arms, though arms we need — not as a call to battle, though embattled we are — but a call to bear the burden of a long twilight struggle, year in and year out, "rejoicing in hope, patient in tribulation" — a struggle against the common enemies of man: tyranny, poverty, disease and war itself.

Can we forge against these enemies a grand and global alliance, north and south, east and west, that can assure a more fruitful life for all mankind? Will you join in that historic effort? . . .

JOHN FITZGERALD KENNEDY

FOR THE RECORD

These were President Kennedy's last official words — the conclusion of the speech he was to have delivered in Dallas:

We in this country, in this generation, are — by destiny rather than choice — the watchmen on the walls of world freedom. We ask therefore, that we may be worthy of our power and responsibility — that we may exercise our strength with wisdom and restraint — and that we may achieve in our time and for all time the ancient vision of peace on earth, good will toward men. That must always be our goal — and the righteousness of our cause must always underlie our strength. For as was written long ago: "Except the Lord keep the city, the watchman waketh but in vain."

JOHN FITZGERALD KENNEDY

LETTER TO PETER CARR, AUGUST 19, 1785

He who permits himself to tell a lie once, finds it much easier to do it a second and third time, till at length it becomes habitual; he tells lies without attending to it, and truths without the world's believing him. This falsehood of the tongue leads to that of the heart, and in time depraves all its good dispositions.

THOMAS JEFFERSON

WRITTEN IN MARCH

The cock is crowing,
The stream is flowing,
The small birds twitter,
The lake doth glitter,
The green field sleeps in the sun:
The oldest and youngest
Are at work with the strongest:
The cattle are grazing,
Their heads never raising,
There are forty feeding like one!

Like an army defeated,
The snow hath retreated,
And now doth fare ill
On the top of the bare hill;
The ploughboy is whooping — anon — anon:
There's joy in the mountains,
There's life in the fountains;
Small clouds are sailing,
Blue sky prevailing,
The rain is over and gone!

WILLIAM WORDSWORTH

THIS MOMENT YEARNING AND THOUGHTFUL

This moment yearning and thoughtful sitting alone,
It seems to me there are other men in other lands
  yearning and thoughtful,
It seems to me I can look over and behold them in
  Germany, Italy, France, Spain,
Or far, far away, in China, or in Russia or Japan,
  talking other dialects,
And it seems to me if I could know those other men
  I should become attached to them as I do to men in
  my own lands.
Oh, I know we should be brethren and lovers, —
I know I should be happy with them.

WALT WHITMAN

ON LIVING*

The riders in a race do not stop short when they reach the goal. There is a little finishing canter before coming to a standstill. There is time to hear the kind voice of friends and to say to one's self: "The work is done." But just as one says that, the answer comes: "The race is over, but the work never is done while the power to work remains." The canter that brings you to a standstill need not be only coming to rest. It cannot be, while you still live. For to live is to function. That is all there is in living.

OLIVER WENDELL HOLMES, JR.

ABRAHAM LINCOLN

This man whose homely face you look upon,
    Was one of nature's masterful, great men:
Born with strong arms, that unfought battles won;
    Direct of speech, and cunning with the pen.
Chosen for large designs, he had the art
    Of winning with his humor, and he went
Straight to his mark, which was the human heart;
    Wise, too, for what he could not break he bent.
Upon his back a more than Atlas-load,
    The burden of the Commonwealth, was laid;
He stooped, and rose up to it, though the road
    Shot suddenly downwards, not a whit dismayed.
Hold, warriors, councillors, kings! All now give place
    To this dear benefactor of the race.

RICHARD HENRY STODDARD

SECOND INAUGURAL ADDRESS

. . . Fondly do we hope — fervently do we pray — that this mighty scourge of war may speedily pass away. Yet, if God wills that it continue until all the wealth piled by the bondsman's two hundred and fifty years of unrequited toil shall be sunk, and until every drop of blood drawn with the lash shall be paid by another drawn with the sword, as was said three thousand years ago, so still it must be said, "The judgments of the Lord are true and righteous altogether."

* From *The Mind and Faith of Justice Holmes* by Max Lerner. Copyright © 1943 by Max Lerner. With permission of Little, Brown and Company.

With malice toward none; with charity for all; with firmness in the right, as God gives us to see the right, let us strive on to finish the work we are in; to bind up the nation's wounds; to care for him who shall have borne the battle, and for his widow, and his orphan — to do all which may achieve and cherish a just and lasting peace among ourselves, and with all nations.

Abraham Lincoln

FOUR DUCKS ON A POND

Four ducks on a pond,
A grass-bank beyond,
A blue sky of spring,
White clouds on the wing —
What a little thing
To remember for years!
To remember with tears!

William Allingham

UP-HILL

Does the road wind up-hill all the way?
  Yes, to the very end.
Will the day's journey take the whole long day?
  From morn to night, my friend.

But is there for the night a resting-place?
  A roof for when the slow dark hours begin.
May not the darkness hide it from my face?
  You cannot miss that inn.

Shall I meet other wayfarers at night?
  Those who have gone before.
Then must I knock or call when just in sight?
  They will not keep you standing at the door.

Shall I find comfort, travel-sore and weak?
  Of labor you shall find the sum.
Will there be beds for me and all who seek?
  Yea, beds for all who come.

Christina Georgina Rossetti

THE INSCRIPTION AT MOUNT VERNON

Washington, the brave, the wise, the good,
Supreme in war, in council, and in peace,
Valiant without ambition, discreet without fear,
Confident without presumption
In disaster, calm; in success, moderate;
  in all, himself.
The hero, the patriot, the Christian.
The father of nations, the friend of mankind,
Who, when he had won all, renounced all,
And sought in the bosom of his family
  and of nature, retirement,
And in the hope of religion, immortality.

◈◈◈

It is always hard to substitute understanding for blaming. It is hard to substitute love for hate. It is hard to put across the idea that we will not solve the problems of peace and war unless we understand ourselves and others. It requires humility, patience, intelligence. But unless we understand how people become friendly or unfriendly, tolerant or intolerant, fearful or courageous, we shall merely muddle around in human relationships.*

EDGAR DALE

From THE CHAMBERED NAUTILUS†

Build thee more stately mansions, O my soul,
  As the swift seasons roll!
  Leave thy low-vaulted past!
Let each new temple, nobler than the last,
Shut thee from heaven with a dome more vast,
  Till thou at length art free,
Leaving thine outgrown shell by life's unresting sea!

OLIVER WENDELL HOLMES

---

* From *The News Letter* (The Ohio State University). Reprinted by permission of Edgar Dale.
† Reprinted by permission of Houghton Mifflin Company.

WINDOWS*

I looked through others' windows
On an enchanted earth,
But out of my own window —
Solitude and dearth.

And yet there is a mystery
I cannot understand —
That others through my window
See an enchanted land.

JESSIE B. RITTENHOUSE

WORK

Let me but do my work from day to day,
In field or forest, at the desk or loom,
In roaring market-place or tranquil room;
Let me but find it in my heart to say,
When vagrant wishes beckon me astray,
"This is my work; my blessing, not my doom;
Of all who live, I am the one by whom
This work can best be done in the right way."

Then shall I see it not too great, nor small,
To suit my spirit and to prove my powers;
Then shall I cheerful greet the labouring hours,
And cheerful turn, when the long shadows fall
At eventide, to play and love and rest,
Because I know for me my work is best.

HENRY VAN DYKE

LINCOLN DEBATES DOUGLAS†

. . . On his head he wore a somewhat battered "stove-pipe" hat. His neck emerged, long and sinewy, from a white collar turned down over a thin black necktie. His lank, ungainly body was clad in a rusty black dress coat with sleeves that should have been longer; but his arms

---

* From *Door of Dreams* by Jessie B. Rittenhouse. Reprinted by permission of Houghton Mifflin Company.

† From *The Autobiography of Carl Schurz,* abridged by Wayne Andrews, with an Introduction by Allan Nevins. (Charles Scribner's Sons, 1961.)

appeared so long that the sleeves of a "store" coat could hardly be expected to cover them all the way down to the wrists. His black trousers, too, permitted a very full view of his large feet. On his left arm he carried a gray woolen shawl, which evidently served him for an overcoat in chilly weather. His left hand held a cotton umbrella of the bulging kind, and also a black satchel that bore the marks of long and hard usage. His right he had kept free for handshaking, of which there was no end until everybody in the car seemed to be satisfied . . .

CARL SCHURZ

LINCOLN DEBATES DOUGLAS*

. . . There was, however, in all he said, a tone of earnest truthfulness, of elevated, noble sentiment, and of kindly sympathy, which added greatly to the strength of his argument, and became, as in the course of his speech he touched upon the moral side of the question in debate, powerfully impressive. Even when attacking his opponent with keen satire or invective, which, coming from any other speaker, would have sounded bitter and cruel, there was still a certain something in his utterance making his hearers feel that those thrusts came from a reluctant heart, and that he would much rather have treated his foe as a friend . . .

CARL SCHURZ

BARTER†

Life has loveliness to sell,
All beautiful and splendid things,
Blue waves whitened on a cliff,
Soaring fire that sways and sings,
And children's faces looking up
Holding wonder like a cup.

Life has loveliness to sell,
Music like a curve of gold,
Scent of pine trees in the rain,
Eyes that love you, arms that hold,
And for your spirit's still delight,
Holy thoughts that star the night.

---

* Ibid.

† Reprinted with permission of The Macmillan Company from *Collected Poems* by Sara Teasdale. Copyright 1917 by The Macmillan Company, renewed 1945 by Mamie T. Wheless.

Spend all you have for loveliness,
Buy it and never count the cost;
For one white singing hour of peace
Count many a year of strife well lost,
And for a breath of ecstasy
Give all you have been, or could be.

SARA TEASDALE

From THE LADDER OF SAINT AUGUSTINE

We have not wings, we cannot soar;
But we have feet to scale and climb
By slow degrees, by more and more,
The cloudy summits of our time.

The mighty pyramids of stone
That wedge-like cleave the desert airs,
When nearer seen, and better known,
Are but gigantic flights of stairs.

The distant mountains, that uprear
Their solid bastions to the skies,
Are crossed by pathways, that appear
As we to higher levels rise.

The heights by great men reached and kept
Were not attained by sudden flight,
But they, while their companions slept,
Were toiling upward in the night.

HENRY WADSWORTH LONGFELLOW

THE FALLING STAR*

I saw a star slide down the sky,
Blinding the north as it went by,
Too burning and too quick to hold,
Too lovely to be bought or sold,
Good only to make wishes on
And then forever to be gone.

SARA TEASDALE

MY LAND IS FAIR FOR ANY EYES TO SEE*

My land is fair for any eyes to see —
Now look, my friends — look to the east and west!
You see the purple hills far in the west —
Hills lined with pine and gum and black-oak tree —
Now to the east you see the fertile valley!
This land is mine, I sing of it to you —
My land beneath the skies of white and blue.
This land is mine, for I am part of it.
I am the land, for it is part of me —
We are akin and this our kinship be!
It would make me a brother to the tree!
And far as eyes can see this land is mine.
Not for one foot of it I have a deed —
To own this land I do not need a deed —
They all belong to me — gum, oak, and pine.

JESSE STUART

◈◈◈

There are moments in our lives, there are moments in a day, when we seem to see beyond the usual. Such are the moments of our greatest happiness. Such are the moments of our greatest wisdom. If one could but recall his vision by some sort of sign. It was in this hope that the arts were invented. Sign-posts on the way to what may be. Sign-posts toward greater knowledge.†

ROBERT HENRI

STARS**

Alone in the night
On a dark hill
With pines around me
Spicy and still,

---

* From the book *Man with a Bull-Tongue Plow* by Jesse Stuart. Copyright © 1934, 1959 by Jesse Stuart *Dutton Paperback Edition*. Reprinted by permission of E. P. Dutton and Company, Inc.

† From *The Art Spirit* by Robert Henri. Copyright 1923 by J. B. Lippincott Company, 1951 by Violet Organ. Reprinted by permission of J. B. Lippincott Company.

** Reprinted with permission of the Macmillan Company from *Flame and Shadow* by Sara Teasdale. Copyright 1920 by The Macmillan Company, renewed 1948 by Mamie T. Wheless.

And a heaven full of stars
Over my head,
White and topaz
And misty red;

Myriads with beating
Hearts of fire
That aeons
Cannot vex or tire;

Up the dome of heaven
Like a great hill,
I watch them marching
Stately and still,

And I know that I
Am honored to be
Witness
Of so much majesty.

SARA TEASDALE

From GOD OF THE OPEN AIR

These are the gifts I ask
Of thee, Spirit serene:
Strength for the daily task,
Courage to face the road.
Good cheer to help me bear the traveller's load,
And, for the hours of rest that come between,
An inward joy in all things heard and seen.
These are the sins I fain
Would have thee take away:
Malice, and cold disdain,
Hot anger, sullen hate,
Scorn of the lowly, envy of the great,
And discontent that casts a shadow gray
On all the brightness of a common day.

HENRY VAN DYKE

LEISURE*

What is this life if, full of care,
We have no time to stand and stare.

No time to stand beneath the boughs
And stare as long as sheep or cows.

No time to see, in broad daylight,
Streams full of stars, like stars at night.

No time to turn at Beauty's glance,
And watch her feet, how they can dance.

No time to wait till her mouth can
Enrich that smile her eyes began.

A poor life this if, full of care,
We have no time to stand and stare.

William Henry Davies

TO THE AMERICAN TROOPS BEFORE THE BATTLE OF LONG ISLAND

The time is now near at hand which must probably determine whether Americans are to be freemen or slaves; whether they are to have any property they can call own; whether their houses and farms are to be pillaged and destroyed, and themselves consigned to a state of wretchedness from which no human efforts will deliver them. The fate of unborn millions will now depend, under God, on the courage and conduct of this army. Our cruel and unrelenting enemy leaves us only the choice of a brave resistance, or the most abject submission. We have, therefore, to resolve to conquer or to die.

George Washington

HOLD FAST YOUR DREAMS*

Within your heart
Keep one still, secret spot
Where dreams may go,
And sheltered so,
May thrive and grow —
Where doubt and fear are not.
Oh, keep a place apart
Within your heart,
For little dreams to go.

LOUISE DRISCOLL

BEAUTY†

Beauty is seen
In the sunlight,
The trees, the birds,
Corn growing and people working
Or dancing for their harvest.

Beauty is heard
In the night,
Wind sighing, rain falling,
Or a singer chanting
Anything in earnest.

Beauty is in yourself.
Good deeds, happy thoughts
That repeat themselves
In your dreams,
In your work,
And even in your rest.

E-YEH-SHURE'

THE RIGHT KIND OF PEOPLE*

Gone is the city, gone the day,
Yet still the story and the meaning stay:
Once where a prophet in the palm shade basked
A traveler chanced at noon to rest his mules.
"What sort of people may they be," he asked,
"In this proud city on the plains o'erspread?"
"Well, friend, what sort of people whence you came?"
"What sort?" the packman scowled; "why, knaves and fools."
"You'll find the people here the same," the wise man said.

Another stranger in the dust drew near,
And pausing, cried, "What sort of people here
In your bright city where yon towers arise?"
"Well, friend, what sort of people whence you came?"
"What sort?" the pilgrim smiled with lifted head;
"Good, true and wise."
"You'll find the people here the same,"
The wise man said.

EDWIN MARKHAM

GIVE ME LIBERTY, OR GIVE ME DEATH!

. . . There is a just God who presides over the destinies of nations; and who will raise up friends to fight our battles for us. The battle, sir, is not to the strong alone; it is to the vigilant, the active, the brave. Besides, sir, we have no election. If we were the base enough to desire it, it is now too late to retire from the contest. There is no retreat, but in submission and slavery! Our chains are forged! Their clanking may be heard on the plains of Boston! The war is inevitable — and let it come! I repeat it, sir, let it come!

It is in vain, sir, to extenuate the matter. Gentlemen may cry, Peace, Peace — but there is no peace. The war is actually begun! The next gale that sweeps from the north will bring to our ears the resounding arms! Our brethren are already in the field! Why stand we here idle? What is it that gentlemen wish? What would they have? Is life so dear, or peace so sweet, as to be purchased at the price of chains and slavery? Forbid it, Almighty God! I know not what course others may take; but as for me, give me liberty, or give me death!

PATRICK HENRY

---

* Reprinted by permission of Virgil Markham.

LAUGH AND BE MERRY*

Laugh and be merry; remember, better the world with a song,
Better the world with a blow in the teeth of a wrong.
Laugh, for the time is brief, a thread the length of a span,
Laugh and be proud to belong to the old proud pageant of man.

Laugh and be merry; remember, in olden time,
God made heaven and earth; for joy He took in a rime,
Made them, and filled them full with the strong red wine of His mirth,
The splendid joy of the stars, the joy of the earth.

So we must laugh and drink from the deep blue cup of the sky,
Join the jubilant song of the great stars sweeping by,
Laugh, and battle, and work, and drink of the wine outpoured
In the dear green earth, the sign of the joy of the Lord.

Laugh and be merry together, like brothers akin,
Guesting awhile in the room of a beautiful inn,
Glad till the dancing stops, and the life of the music ends.
Laugh till the game is played; and be you merry, my friends.

John Masefield

DUST OF SNOW†

The way a crow
Shook down on me
The dust of snow
From a hemlock tree

Has given my heart
A change of mood
And saved some part
Of a day I had rued.

Robert Frost

* Reprinted with permission of The Macmillan Company from *Collected Poems* by John Masefield. Copyright 1912 by The Macmillan Company, renewed 1940 by John Masefield.

† From *Complete Poems of Robert Frost*. Copyright 1916, 1923, 1928 by Holt, Rinehart and Winston, Inc. Copyright 1944, 1951, © 1956 by Robert Frost. Reprinted by permission of Holt, Rinehart and Winston, Inc.

THE ROAD NOT TAKEN*

Two roads diverged in a yellow wood,
And sorry I could not travel both
And be one traveler, long I stood
And looked down one as far as I could
To where it bent in the undergrowth;

Then took the other, as just as fair,
And having perhaps the better claim,
Because it was grassy and wanted wear;
Though as for that the passing there
Had worn them really about the same,

And both that morning equally lay
In leaves no step had trodden black.
Oh, I kept the first for another day!
Yet knowing how way leads on to way,
I doubted if I should ever come back.

I shall be telling this with a sigh
Somewhere ages and ages hence:
Two roads diverged in a wood, and I —
I took the one less traveled by,
And that has made all the difference.

ROBERT FROST

THE COIN†

Into my heart's treasury
I slipped a coin
That time cannot take
Nor a thief purloin —
Oh, better than the minting
Of a gold-crowned king
Is the safe-kept memory
Of a lovely thing.

SARA TEASDALE

OPPORTUNITY

They do me wrong, who say I come no more
When once I knock and fail to find you in;
For every day I stand outside your door
And bid you wake, and rise to fight and win.

Weep not for precious chances passed away!
Weep not for golden ages on the wane!
Each night I burn the records of the day —
At sunrise each soul is born again.

WALTER MALONE

EVERYONE SANG*

Everyone suddenly burst out singing;
And I was filled with such delight
As prisoned birds must find in freedom,
Winging wildly across the white
Orchards and dark green fields; on, on, and out of sight.

Everyone's voice was suddenly lifted,
And beauty came like the setting sun.
My heart was shaken with tears, and horror
Drifted away . . . O but everyone
Was a bird; and the song was wordless; the singing
will never be done.

SIEGFRIED SASSOON

STOPPING BY WOODS ON A SNOWY EVENING†

Whose woods these are I think I know.
His house is in the village though;
He will not see me stopping here
To watch his woods fill up with snow.

My little horse must think it queer
To stop without a farmhouse near
Between the woods and frozen lake
The darkest evening of the year.

He gives his harness bells a shake
To ask if there is some mistake.
The only other sound's the sweep
Of easy wind and downy flake.

The woods are lovely, dark and deep,
But I have promises to keep,
And miles to go before I sleep,
And miles to go before I sleep.

ROBERT FROST

LOVELIEST OF TREES*

Loveliest of trees, the cherry now
Is hung with bloom along the bough,
And stands about the woodland ride
Wearing white for Eastertide.

Now, of my threescore years and ten,
Twenty will not come again,
And take from seventy springs a score,
It only leaves me fifty more.

And since to look at things in bloom
Fifty springs are little room,
About the woodlands I will go
To see the cherry hung will snow.

A. E. HOUSMAN

* From *A Shropshire Lad* — Authorized Edition — from *The Collected Poems* of A. E. Housman.

INDIAN*

I don't know who this Indian is,
A bow within his hand,
But he is hiding by a tree
And watching white men land.
They may be gods — they may be fiends —
They certainly look rum.
He wonders who on earth they are
And why on earth they've come.

He knows his streams are full of fish,
His forests full of deer,
And his tribe is the mighty tribe
That all the others fear.
— And, when the French or English land,
The Spanish or the Dutch,
They'll tell him they're the mighty tribe
And no one else is much.

They'll kill his deer and net his fish
And clear away his wood,
And frequently remark to him
They do it for his good.
Then he will scalp and he will shoot
And he will burn and slay
And break the treaties he has made
— And, children, so will they.

We won't go into all of that
For it's too long a story,
And some is brave and some is sad
And nearly all is gory.
But, just remember this about
Our ancestors so dear:
They didn't find an empty land.
The Indians were here.

ROSEMARY AND STEPHEN VINCENT BENÉT

---

* From *A Book of Americans* by Rosemary and Stephen Vincent Benét, published by Holt, Rinehart and Winston, Inc. Copyright 1933 by Stephen Vincent Benét. Copyright renewed © 1961 by Rosemary Carr Benét.

HOW DO WE RECOGNIZE PREJUDICE?
WHAT CAN WE DO ABOUT IT?*

We are prejudiced

IF we believe that our race is born with more ability, more brains and character, than other races

OR

IF we think that members of our own church are good and most others queer or bad

OR

IF we ever accuse a whole group of people of anything

OR

IF we repeat rumors or gossip about other groups

OR

IF we believe members of some groups should stay out of certain jobs and schools

OR

IF we keep our children or friends from associating with members of other races and creeds

BUT

We are people of good will

IF we judge every person by his own record

AND

IF we believe that all groups are born with the same ability and can make good if they have equal chances

AND

IF we make friends with members of all groups

AND

IF we stop rumors and gossip about whole groups

AND

IF we work for a square deal in jobs, votes, homes and schools for everybody

AND

IF we admit the many gifts made by all groups to our own welfare

---

* Reprinted by permission of The National Conference of Christians and Jews, Inc.

BUT

What Causes Prejudice and What Can We Do About IT?

We are prejudiced

BECAUSE we don't know the truth about other groups

AND

BECAUSE we have pictures-in-the-head about other groups, which are false

AND

BECAUSE we think a whole group is like a few of its bad actors we know or hear about

AND

BECAUSE we listen to gossip and rumors which are spread by propagandists for their own profit and power

AND

BECAUSE we blame other people for our own troubles and failures

AND

BECAUSE we are afraid that others may grab our jobs or outvote us or drag down our neighborhoods

AND

BECAUSE we are so cocky about our own groups that we think all others are no good

BUT

We can build good will

BY judging each person on his own record

AND

BY having good friends in all racial and religious groups

AND

BY learning the truth about all groups

AND

BY knowing how much all groups have done to help make our country free and prosperous

AND

BY getting our churches and clubs to do things with other churches and groups

AND

BY seeing that every person has the same rights and opportunities that we want for ourselves

AND

BY working for good jobs, good homes and good schools for everybody

AND

BY working for good government which will guarantee liberty and justice for all

If we are prejudiced and intolerant

WE ARE NOT HAPPY
WE ARE NOT SCIENTIFIC
WE ARE NOT RELIGIOUS
WE ARE NOT AMERICAN

If we understand and respect people of all kinds

WE ARE HAPPY
WE ARE SCIENTIFIC
WE ARE RELIGIOUS
WE ARE AMERICAN

WILLARD JOHNSON

OUTWITTED*

He drew a circle that shut me out —
Heretic, rebel, a thing to flout.
But Love and I had the wit to win:
We drew a circle that took him in!

EDWIN MARKHAM

LIFETIME READING PLAN†

Most of us have a Lifetime Savings Plan. We don't like to go along life's road with nothing in our pockets. But how about going along it with nothing in our minds.

The man I pity most is the one who experiences this wonderful world, and leaves it without ever quite knowing what his life has been about. Whatever the state of his bank account, he lives and dies mentally bankrupt.

So set yourself a Lifetime Reading Plan! Such a grand design can fill your mind, slowly, gradually, year by year over the whole of your life, with what the greatest writers of our Western civilization have thought and felt.

---

* From *Shoes of Happines and Other Poems* by Erwin Markham. Reprinted by permission of Virgil Markham.

† Reprinted from *This Week* Magazine. Copyright 1959 by the United Newspapers Magazine Corporation. Developed in detail in *The Lifetime Reading Plan* by Clifton Fadiman, published and available in hard cover by World Publishing Company, in paperback by Avon, in paperback by Forum Books. Used by permission of Edwin Fadiman and *This Week* Magazine.

The contemporary man who has shared these thoughts and feelings will understand how he has emerged out of 3000 years of history. He will know how he got the ideas by which he lives. He will feel buoyed up by the great and noble stream of Western civilization of which he is a part.

Books are only one key to these discoveries. But the wisest men agree that they are probably the best key. Enjoy them. There's nothing solemn about feeling your mind stretch. It's the most rewarding feeling in the world. These books are an adventure. Reading is not a passive experience — unless you're reading trash. It can be one of the most vigorous forms of living. A good book, like healthy exercise, can give you that pleasant sense of fatigue which comes of having stretched your mental muscles.

"He that loves reading has everything within his reach." — William Godwin.

CLIFTON FADIMAN

From IT'S FUN TO READ*

Reading is like eating peanuts: once you begin, you tend to go on and on. Every book stands by itself, like a one-family house, but books are like houses in a city. Although they are separate, together they all add up to something; they are connected with each other and with other cities. The same ideas, or related ones, turn up in different places; the human problems that repeat themselves in life repeat themselves in literature, but with different solutions according to different authors who wrote at different times. Books influence each other; they link the past and the present and the future and have their own generations, like families. Wherever you start reading you connect yourself with one of the families of ideas, and, in the long run, you not only find out about the world and the people in it; you find out about yourself, too.

BENNETT CERF

* From *The Wonderful World of Books* edited by Alfred Stefferud. Copyright © 1952 by Alfred Stefferud. *The Wonderful World of Books* is a joint publication of Houghton Mifflin Company and The New American Library, Inc.

◈◈◈

The moving words below beautifully express our ideals of equality and the brotherhood of man. They are from a memorial address given by Rabbi Roland B. Gittelsohn in March 1945. He dedicated a cemetery for the marines who fell in the battle for the Japanese-held island of Iwo Jima in World War II.

> Here lie men who loved America because their ancestors generations ago helped in her founding, and other men who loved her with equal passion because they themselves or their own fathers escaped from oppression to her blessed shores. Here lie officers and men, Negroes and whites, rich men and poor — together. Here are Protestants, Catholics, and Jews — together. Here no man prefers another because of his faith or despises him because of his color. Here there are no quotas of how many from each group are admitted or allowed. Among these men there is no discrimination. No prejudice. No hatred. Theirs is the highest and purest democracy.*

RABBI ROLAND B. GITTELSOHN

From THE LAY OF THE LAST MINSTREL

Breathes there the man, with soul so dead
Who never to himself hath said,
  This is my own, my native land!
Whose heart hath ne'er within him burn'd
As home his footsteps he hath turn'd,
  From wandering on a foreign strand?
If such there breathe, go, mark him well;
For him no minstrel raptures swell;
High though his titles, proud his name,
Boundless his wealth as wish can claim, —
Despite those titles, power, and pelf,
The wretch, concentred all in self,
  Living, shall forfeit fair renown,
And, doubly dying, shall go down
To the vile dust, from whence he sprung,
Unwept, unhonour'd, and unsung.

SIR WALTER SCOTT

* Reprinted by permission of Rabbi Roland B. Gittelsohn.

THE FALL OF THE ALAMO

Fellow Citizens and Compatriots: I am besieged with a thousand or more of the Mexicans under Santa Anna. I have sustained a continual bombardment and cannonade for 24 hours and have not lost a man. The enemy has demanded a surrender at discretion; otherwise, the garrison are to be put to the sword, if the fort is taken. I have answered the demand with a cannon shot, and our flag still waves proudly from the walls. *I shall never surrender or retreat.* Then, I call on you in the name of Liberty, of patriotism and everything dear to the American character, to come to our aid with all dispatch. The enemy is receiving reinforcements daily and will no doubt increase to three or four thousand in four or five days. If this call is neglected I am determined to sustain myself as long as possible and die like a soldier who never forgets what is due to his own honor and that of his country. VICTORY or DEATH.

COLONEL WILLIAM BARRET TRAVIS

◈◈◈

Be courteous to all, but intimate with few, and let those few be well tried before you give them your confidence. True friendship is a plant of slow growth, and must undergo and withstand the shocks of adversity before it is entitled to the appellation.

GEORGE WASHINGTON

From FAREWELL ADDRESS, SEPTEMBER 17, 1796

Observe good faith and justice toward all nations. Cultivate peace and harmony with all . . . The nation which indulges toward another an habitual hatred or an habitual fondness is in some degree a slave. It is a slave to its animosity or to its affection, either of which is sufficient to lead it astray from its duty and its interest.

GEORGE WASHINGTON

BE STRONG

Be strong!
We are not here to play, to dream, to drift;
We have hard work to do, and loads to lift;
Shun not the struggle — face it; 'tis God's gift.

Be strong!
Say not, "The days are evil. Who's to blame?"
And fold the hands and acquiesce — oh shame!
Stand up, speak out, and bravely, in God's name.

Be strong!
It matters not how deep intrenched the wrong,
How hard the battle goes, the day how long;
Faint not — fight on! Tomorrow comes the song.

MALTBIE DAVENPORT BABCOCK

HUMAN DIGNITY*

There are few things will earn you the respect of others quite so surely as personal dignity. You don't have to be pompous or glum to be dignified. You simply have to respect yourself — and others — and behave accordingly. After all, you represent the noblest creation yet seen on earth. Why not act the part?

A famous French writer once took a long look at life and concluded, "The only goal of man should be the attainment of human dignity, with all its implications. In other words, all his intellectual acquisitions, all the facilities which society puts at his disposal — the schools, universities, libraries, laboratories; all those offered by religion; all the occasions given him to develop his own aptitudes, his work, his leisure, must be considered as tools destined to improve his personality, his moral self and to make it progress." The "attainment of human dignity" is a personal challenge!

ME†

As long as I live
I shall always be
My Self — and no other,
Just me.

Like a tree —
Willow, elder,
Aspen, thorn,
Or cypress forlorn.

---

* From *"Gaylord's Triangle,"* February 1965. Used with permission.
† From *Bells and Grass* by Walter de la Mare. Copyright 1942 by Walter de la Mare. Reprinted by permission of The Viking Press, Inc.

Like a flower,
For its hour —
Primrose, or pink,
Or a violet —
Sunned by the sun.
And with dewdrops wet.

Always just me.
Till the day come on
When I leave this body,
It's all then done,
And the spirit within it
Is gone.

WALTER DE LA MARE

THANKSGIVING DAY PROCLAMATION, OCTOBER 28, 1961

. . . More than three centuries ago, the Pilgrims, after a year of hardship and peril, humbly and reverently set aside a special day upon which to give thanks to God for their preservation and for the good harvest from the virgin soil upon which they had labored. Grave and unknown dangers remained. Yet by their faith and by their toil they had survived the rigors of the harsh New England winter. Hence they paused in their labors to give thanks for the blessings that had been bestowed upon them by Divine Providence.

This year, as the harvest draws near its close and the year approaches its end, awesome perils again remain to be faced. Yet we have, as in the past, ample reason to be thankful for the abundance of our blessings. We are grateful for the blessings of faith and health and strength and for the imperishable spiritual gifts of love and hope. We give thanks, too, for our freedom as a nation; for the strength of our arms and the faith of our friends; for the beliefs and confidence we share; for our determination to stand firmly for what we believe to be right and to resist mightily what we believe to be base; and for the heritage of liberty bequeathed by our ancestors which we are priviliged to preserve for our children and our children's children . . .

Let us observe this day with reverence and with prayer that will rekindle in us the will and show us the way not only to preserve our blessings, but also to extend them to the four corners of the earth. Let us by our example, as well as by our material aid, assist all peoples of all nations who are striving to achieve a better life in freedom.

JOHN FITZGERALD KENNEDY

DREAMS*

Hold fast to dreams
For if dreams die
Life is a broken-winged bird
That cannot fly.

Hold fast to dreams
For when dreams go
Life is a barren field
Frozen with snow.

LANGSTON HUGHES

WISDOM†

I stand most humbly
Before man's wisdom,
Knowing we are not
Really wise:

If we were
We'd open up the kingdom
And make earth happy
As the dreamed of skies.

LANGSTON HUGHES

From THE SPIRIT OF AMERICA**

Ahead are the children of the next generation. We are to carry to them the Spirit of America. We must show them what went before, what lies ahead. We must lead them to seek through the dimness of centuries, a gleaming line of silver white. It is the line of the Crusaders, steady, straight and strong, the quest for the Holy Grail, the search for Freedom.

Back there, glimmering faintly in the dawn of history stand the gods, their very names lost in the long ago.

There are the prophets, and the teachers, and the lawgivers, a mighty host.

There is Moses, and those who followed him out of bondage.

There are the martyrs.

Now the line brightens and broadens. We are nearer. We can see some of the faces. There are Columbus, Washington, Lafayette, Garibaldi.

There is Lincoln.

There is Roosevelt.

There are the countless hosts who fought on the world's battlefields. We know them well.

The light streams from their faces. Their helmets gleam. Their swords flash fire. A fearless, dauntless, invincible army they march on, and on and on to the fullness of Freedom. They live.

They are with us children of America. They urge us on. They command us to go forward.

Man has slaved through the ages that we might be free. He has battled that we might have peace. He has studied that we might know. He has left us the heritage of the ages that we in our turn might carry it on.

Ahead of us are the children of the next generation. It is for them that we live. It is for them that we must go on.

We are the torchbearers of Liberty. We, too, must take our place in the search for Freedom, the Quest for the Holy Grail.

It is for this, we the children of America were born.

ANGELO PATRI

From FREEDOM FROM FEAR*

A hundred and sixty odd years ago, we, as a nation, asserted that all men were created equal, that all men were entitled to life, liberty and the pursuit of happiness. Those were large assertions, but we have tried to live up to them. We have not always succeeded, we have often failed. But our will and desire as a nation have been to live up to them.

Now, in concert with other free nations, we say that those children you see and other children like them all over the world shall grow to manhood and womanhood free from fear. We say that neither their minds nor their bodies shall be cramped or distorted or broken by tyranny and oppression. We say they shall have a chance, and an equal chance, to grow and develop and lead the lives they choose to lead, not lives mapped out for them by a master. And we say that freedom for ourselves involves freedom for others — that it is a universal right, neither lightly given by providence nor to be maintained by words alone, but by acts and deeds and living.

We who are alive today did not make our free institutions. We got

* *Freedom from Fear* by Stephen Vincent Benét. Copyright, 1943, by The Curtis Publishing Company. Reprinted by permission of Brand and Brand.

them from the men of the past and we hold them in trust for the future. Should we put ease and selfishness above them, that trust will fail and we shall lose all, not a portion or a degree of liberty, but all that has been built for us and all that we hope to build. Real peace will not be won with one victory. It can be won only by long determination, firm resolve and a wish to share and work with other men, no matter what their race or creed or condition. And yet, we do have the choice. We can have freedom from fear.

STEPHEN VINCENT BENÉT

◈◈◈

It is not growing like a tree
In bulk, doth make man better be;
Or standing long an oak, three hundred year,
To fall a log at last, dry, bald, and sear:
A lily of a day
Is fairer far in May,
Although it fall and die that night, —
It was the plant and flower of Light.
In small proportions we just beauties see,
And in short measures life may perfect be.

BEN JONSON

SKY-BORN MUSIC

Let me go where'er I will
I hear a sky-born music still;
It sounds from all things old,
It sounds from all things young;
From all that's fair, from all that's foul,
Peals out a cheerful song.
It is not only in the rose,
It is not only in the bird,
Not only where the rainbow glows,
Nor in the song of woman heard,
But in the darkest, meanest things
There always, always something sings.
'Tis not in the high stars alone,
Nor in the cups of budding flowers,
Nor in the redbreast's mellow tone,
Nor in the bow that smiles in showers,
But in the mud and scum of things
There always, always something sings.

RALPH WALDO EMERSON

POETRY AND PROSE

Grades 10—12

THE GOVERNMENT OF THE UNITED STATES GIVES TO BIGOTRY NO SANCTION

(From his letter to the Hebrew Congregation in Newport, Rhode Island)

The Citizens of the United States of America have a right to applaud themselves for having given mankind examples of an enlarged and liberal policy: a policy worthy of imitation. All possess alike liberty of conscience and immunities of citizenship. It is now no more that toleration is spoken of, as if it was by the indulgence of one class of people that another enjoyed the exercise of their inherent natural rights. For happily the Government of the United States, which gives to bigotry no sanction, to persecution no assistance, requires only that they who live under its protection should demean themselves as good citizens in giving it on all occasions their effectual support.

GEORGE WASHINGTON

From STANZAS ON FREEDOM

They are slaves who fear to speak,
For the fallen and the weak;
They are slaves who will not choose,
Hatred, scoffing, and abuse;
Rather than in silence shrink,
From the truth they needs must think;
They are slaves who dare not be,
In the right with two or three.

JAMES RUSSELL LOWELL

A SCHOOL CODE ON TOLERANCE

I will never knowingly, by word or deed, injure anyone's person, feelings, or property in any manner.

I will always respect the religious beliefs of others as I respect my own.

I will show courtesy to other people at all times, particularly to my elders.

I will abide by the laws and regulations of my school and community.

I will be honest with myself and others, and I will practice cleanliness of mind and body at all times.

PUPILS OF NEW YORK CITY PUBLIC SCHOOLS

THE NEW COLOSSUS

(Written in 1883. The Statue of Liberty was unveiled in 1866)

Not like the brazen giant of Greek fame,
With conquering limbs astride from land to land;
Here at our sea-washed, sunset gates shall stand
A mighty woman with a torch, whose flame
Is the imprisoned lightning, and her name
Mother of Exiles. From her beacon-hand
Glows world-wide welcome; her mild eyes command
The air-bridged harbor that twin cities frame.
"Keep, ancient lands, your storied pomp!" cries she
With silent lips. "Give me your tired, your poor,
Your huddled masses yearning to breathe free,
The wretched refuse of your teeming shore.
Send these, the homeless, tempest-tossed to me,
I lift my lamp beside the golden door!"

EMMA LAZARUS

From THE AMERICAN CRISIS

These are the times that try men's souls. The summer soldier and the sunshine patriot will, in this crisis, shrink from the service of their country; but he that stands it *now*, deserves the love and thanks of man and woman. Tyranny, like hell, is not easily conquered; yet we have this consolation with us, that the harder the conflict, the more glorious the triumph. What we obtain too cheap, we esteem too lightly; it is dearness only that gives everything its value. Heaven knows how to put a proper price upon its goods; and it would be strange, indeed, if so celestial an article as FREEDOM should not be highly rated.

THOMAS PAINE

From THE LINCOLN-DOUGLAS DEBATES

. . . It is the eternal struggle between these two principles — right and wrong — throughout the world. They are the two principles that have stood face to face from the beginning of time and will ever continue to struggle. The one is the common right of humanity, and the other the divine right of kings. It is the same principle in whatever shape it develops itself. It is the same spirit that says, "You toil and work and earn bread, and I will eat it." No matter in what shape it comes, whether from the mouth of a king who seeks to bestride the people of his own nation and live from the fruit of their labor, or from one race of men as an apology for enslaving another race, it is the same tyrannical principle.

ABRAHAM LINCOLN

From THE LINCOLN-DOUGLAS DEBATES

In his final words tonight the Judge said that we may be "the terror of the world." I don't think we want to be that. I think we would prefer to be the encouragement of the world, the proof that man is at last worthy to be free. But — we shall provide no such encouragement unless we can establish our ability as a nation to live and grow. And we shall surely do neither if these states fail to remain *united*. There can be no distinction in the definitions of liberty, as between one section and another, one race and another, one class and another. "A house divided against itself cannot stand." This government cannot endure permanently half *slave* and half *free*!

ABRAHAM LINCOLN

From ADDRESS, FEBRUARY 22, 1861

I have never had a feeling, politically, that did not spring from the sentiments embodied in the Declaration of Independence. I have often pondered over the dangers which were incurred by the men who assembled here and framed and adopted that Declaration. I have pondered over the toils that were endured by the officers and soldiers of the army who achieved that independence. I have often inquired of myself what great principle or idea it was that kept this Confederacy so long together. It was not the mere matter of separation of the colonies from the motherland, but that sentiment in the Declaration of Independence which gave liberty not alone to the people of this country, but hope to all the world, for all future time.

ABRAHAM LINCOLN

LETTER TO A FRIEND

(Written in A.D. 1513)

I salute you. I am your friend and my love for you goes deep. There is nothing I can give you which you have not got; but there is much, very much, that, while I cannot give it, you can take.

No Heaven can come to us unless our hearts find rest in today. Take Heaven! No peace lies in the future which is not hidden in this present little instance. Take Peace! The gloom of the world is but a shadow. Behind it, yet within our reach, is Joy. There is radiance and glory in the darkness, could we but see — and to see we have only to look. I beseech you to look.

Life is so generous a giver, but we, judging its gifts by their covering, cast them away as ugly or heavy or hard. Remove the covering and you will find beneath it a living splendor, woven of love, by wisdom, with power.

Welcome it, grasp it, and you touch the Angel's hand that brings it to you. Everything we call a trial or a sorrow or a duty, believe me, that Angel's hand is there; the gift is there, and the wonder of an overshadowing presence. Our joys too: be not content with them as joys. They too conceal diviner gifts.

Life is so full of meaning and purpose, so full of beauty — beneath its covering — that you will find earth but cloaks your heaven. Courage then to claim it, that is all! But courage you have, and the knowledge that we are pilgrims together, wending through unknown country, home.

And so, at this Christmas time, I greet you. No quite as the world sends greetings, but with profound esteem and with the prayer that for you, now and forever, the day breaks, and the shadows flee away.

FRA GIOVANNI

THE COMFORT OF FRIENDS

They that love beyond the world cannot be separated by it.

Death cannot kill what never dies.

Nor can spirits ever be divided that love and live in the same divine principle; the root and record of their friendship.

If absence be not death, neither is theirs.

Death is but crossing the world, as friends do the seas; they live in one another still.

For they must needs be present, that love and live in that which is Omni-present.

In this divine glass they see face to face; and their converse is free as well as pure.

This is the comfort of friends, that though they may be said to die, yet their friendship and society are, in the best sense, ever present, because immortal.

WILLIAM PENN

THE JOY OF WORK

Give us, oh, give us, the man who sings at his work! He will do more in the same time, — he will do it better, — he will persevere longer. One is scarcely sensible of fatigue whilst he marches to music. The very stars are said to make harmony as they revolve in their spheres. Wondrous is the strength of cheerfulness, altogether past calculation in its powers of endurance. Efforts, to be permanently useful, must be uniformly joyous, a spirit all sunshine, graceful from very gladness, beautitful because bright.

THOMAS CARLYLE

THE SALUTATION OF THE DAWN

Listen to the exhortation of the dawn!
Look to this day! For it is life,
  The very life of life.
In its brief course lie all the varieties
And realities of your existence.
  The bliss of growth,
  The glory of action,
  The splendor of beauty,
For yesterday is but a dream,
And tomorrow is only a vision;
  But today well lived
Makes every yesterday a dream of happiness,
And every tomorrow a vision of hope.
Look well, therefore, to this day!
Such is the salutation of the dawn.

ANONYMOUS

THE INNER MAN*

We do not know a nation until we know its pleasures of life, just as we do not know a man until we know how he spends his leisure. It is when a man ceases to do the things he has to do, and does the things he likes to do, that the character is revealed. It is when the repressions of society and business are gone and when the goads of money and fame and ambition are lifted, and man's spirit wanders where it listeth, that we see the inner man, his real self.

LIN YUTANG

* From *My Country and My People* by Lin Yutang. Reprinted by permission of Lin Yutang.

THE INSCRIPTION ON PLYMOUTH ROCK MONUMENT, MASSACHUSETTS

This monument marks the first burying ground in Plymouth of the passengers of the Mayflower. Here, under cover of darkness, the fast dwindling company laid their dead, leveling the earth above them lest the Indians should learn how many were the graves. History records no nobler venture for faith and freedom than of this Pilgrim band. In weariness and painfulness, in watching often in hunger and cold, they laid the foundation of a state wherein every man through countless ages should have liberty to worship God in his own way. May their example inspire thee to do thy part in perpetuating and spreading the lofty ideals of our republic throughout the world.

They laid the foundation of a state wherein every man through countless ages should have liberty.

BOOKS

Consider what you have in the smallest chosen library. A company of the wisest and wittiest men that could be picked out of all civil countries, in a thousand years, have set in best order the results of their learning and wisdom. The men themselves were hid and inaccessible, solitary, impatient of interruption, fenced by etiquette; but the thought which they did not uncover to their bosom friend is here written out in transparent words to us, the strangers of another age.

RALPH WALDO EMERSON

Let me warn you this: the king who values his throne, nay, his very life, will grant his subjects the utmost freedom within reason, for there is no man so dangerous as he whose rights have been taken from him, whose will has been subjugated, and whose life has been altered to suit him who calls himself "master." It is not in the nature of man to live but as himself, and the sovereign who seeks to take from him this essential of natural being will find one day that he has created not a willing slave but a monster of vengeance.

ANONYMOUS

From WALDEN

I learned this, at least, by my experiment: that if one advances confidently in the direction of his dreams, and endeavors to live the life which he has imagined, he will meet with a success unexpected in common hours. He will put some things behind, will pass an invisible boundary; new, universal, and more liberal laws will begin to establish themselves around and within him; or the old laws be expanded, and interpreted in his favor in a more liberal sense, and he will live with the license of a higher order of beings. In proportion as he simplifies his life, the laws of the universe will appear less complex, and solitude will not be solitude, nor poverty poverty, nor weakness weakness. If you have built castles in the air, your work need not be lost; that is where they should be. Now put the foundations under them.

HENRY THOREAU

HOW I FOUND PEACE*

"This above all: to thine own self be true;
And it must follow, as the night the day,
Thou canst not then be false to any man."

WILLIAM SHAKESPEARE

For more than fifty years as a reporter, editor, and radio commentator, I have tried to live up to this bit of good counsel with which Polonius sent Laertes on his way.

Every man sets himself a certain standard; the hard thing is to live up to it. In my line of work, that of analyzing and interpreting the news of the day for millions of readers and listeners, the temptation to serve something other than the public interest is constant. The human instinct to protect friends, the natural desire to escape criticism, the direct or indirect pressure from business and editorial associates, the more or less legitimate demands of an advertising sponsor are always raising ethical issues.

Without some guiding principle it is not easy to know what to do. The simplest way out is to yield to pressure. But that undermines character and makes it more difficult to resist the next demand.

As a boy I studied the lives of our great American editors and learned that they became great because they had the courage and independence to be true to themselves. That became my ambition: to make the public cause my cause and to serve it regardless of cost or consequence. I have not always been right, alas, but I have been true to myself even when I was wrong. And, for half a century, I have had peace of mind.

H. V. KALTENBORN

---

* From *New Treasury of Words to Live By* by William I. Nichols, ed. Copyright 1959 by Simon and Schuster, Inc. and reprinted with their permission.

THANKSGIVING

In his first year as President, George Washington issued the following proclamation:

Whereas it is the duty of all Nations to acknowledge the providence of Almighty God, to obey His will, to be grateful for His benefits, and humbly to implore His protection, and favors . . . Now, therefore, I do recommend and assign Thursday . . . next, to be devoted by the People of these States to the service of that great and glorious Being, who is the Beneficent Author of all the good that was, that is, or that will be; that we may then all unite in rendering unto Him our sincere and humble thanks for His kind care and protection of the people of this country . . . and for all the great and various favors which He has been pleased to confer upon us.

THREE THINGS COME NOT BACK

Remember THREE THINGS come not back;
The arrow sent upon its track —
It will not swerve, it will not stay
Its speed; it flies to wound, or slay.

The spoken word so soon forgot
By thee; but it has perished not;
In other hearts 'tis living still
And doing work for good or ill.

AND THE LOST OPPORTUNITY
That cometh back *no more* to thee,
In vain thou weepest, in vain dost yearn
Those three will nevermore return.

ANONYMOUS

THE FOUR FREEDOMS

(From Franklin Delano Roosevelt's Annual Message to Congress, 1941)

In the future days, which we seek to make secure, we look forward to a world founded upon four essential human freedoms.

The first is freedom of speech and expression — everywhere in the world.

The second is freedom of every person to worship God in his own way — everywhere in the world.

The third is freedom from want — which, translated into world terms, means economic understandings which will secure to every nation a healthy peacetime life for its inhabitants — everywhere in the world.

The fourth is the freedom from fear — which, translated into world terms, means a world-wide reduction of armaments to such a point and in such a thorough fashion that no nation will be in a position to commit an act of physical aggression against any neighbor — anywhere in the world.

THE ATHENIAN OATH

We will never bring disgrace on this, our city, by an act of dishonesty or cowardice, and never desert our suffering comrades in the ranks.

We will fight for the ideals and sacred things of the city, both alone and with many.

We will revere and obey the city's laws, and we will do our best to incite a like respect and reverence in those above us who are prone to annul them and set them at naught.

We will strive unceasingly to quicken the public's sense of public duty; that thus in all these ways we may transmit this city, not less, but greater, better and more beautiful than it was transmitted to us.

THE BIRD LET LOOSE

The bird let loose in eastern skies,
  When hastening fondly home,
Ne'er stoops to earth her wing, nor flies
  Where idle warblers roam;
But high she shoots through air and light,
  Above all low delay,
Where nothing earthly bounds her flight,
  Nor shadow dims her way.

So grant me, God, from every care
And stain of passion free,
Aloft, through Virtue's purer air,
To hold my course to thee!
No sin to cloud, no lure to stay
My soul, as home she springs; —
Thy sunshine on her joyful way,
Thy freedom in her wings!

THOMAS MOORE

PATRIOTS OF MANKIND

Are we not all of race divine,
Alike of an immortal line?
Shall man to man afford derision
But for some casual division?
To malice and to mischief prone,
From climate, canton, and from zone,
Parties and distinction make
For parties' and distinction's sake?
Souls sprung from an ethereal flame,
However clad, are still the same;
Nor should we judge the heart or head
By air we breathe, or earth we tread.
Give prejudices to the wind,
And let's be patriots of mankind.

CHRISTOPHER SMART

WHAT IS A MAN PROFITED?*

The other day in Emporia, the longest funeral procession that has formed in ten years followed the Rev. John Jones three long miles in the hot July sun out to Dry Creek Cemetery. Now, a funeral procession may mean little or much. When a rich and powerful man dies, the people play politics and attend his funeral for various reasons. But here was the body of a meek, gentle little old man — a man "without purse or scrip." It won't take twenty minutes to settle his estate in probate court. He was a preacher of the gospel — but preachers have been buried before this in Emporia without much show of sorrow.

The reason so many people lined up behind the hearse that held the kind old man's mortality was simple: they loved him. He devoted his

* Reprinted by permission of W. L. White.

life to helping people. In a very simple way, without money or worldly power, he gave of the gentleness of his heart to all around him. We are apt to say that money talks, but it speaks a broken, poverty-stricken language. Hearts talk better, clearer, and with a wider intelligence. This old man with the soft voice and the kindly manners knew the language of the heart and he spoke it where it would give zest to joy. He worked manfully and with a will in his section of the vineyard, and against odds and discouragements he won time and again. He was infinitely patient and brave. He held a simple, old-fashioned faith in God and his lovind kindness.

When others gave money — which was of their store — he gave prayers and hard work and an inspiring courage. He helped. In his sphere he was power. And so when he lay down to sleep hundreds of friends trudged out to bid him good-by with moist eyes and with cramped throats to wish him slumber.

And then they turned back to the world to make money — to make money — what a hollow impotent thing! What is a man profited if he gain the whole world and lose his own soul!

WILLIAM ALLEN WHITE

MY SYMPHONY

To live content with small means; to seek elegance rather than luxury; and refinement rather than fashion; to be worthy, not respectable; and wealthy, not rich; to study hard, think quietly, talk gently, act frankly; to listen to stars and birds, to babes and sages, with open heart; to bear all cheerfully, do all bravely, await occasion, hurry never; in a word, to let the spiritual, unbidden and unconscious grow up through the common. This is to be my symphony.

WILLIAM ELLERY CHANNING

From THE SPIRIT OF LIBERTY*

. . . What then is the spirit of liberty? I cannot define it; I can only tell you my own faith. The spirit of liberty is the spirit which is not too sure that it is right; the spirit of liberty is the spirit which seeks to understand the minds of other men and women; the spirit of liberty is the

* Reprinted by permission of Alfred A. Knopf, Inc. from *The Spirit of Liberty*; Papers and Addresses of Learned Hand, edited by Irving Dilliard.

spirit which weighs their interests alongside its own without bias; the spirit of liberty remembers that not even a sparrow falls to earth unheeded; the spirit of liberty is the spirit of Him who, near two thousand years ago, taught mankind that lesson it has never learned, but has never quite forgotten; that there may be a kingdom where the least shall be heard and considered side by side with the greatest. And now in that spirit, that spirit of an America which has never been, and which may never be; nay, which never will be except as the conscience and the courage of Americans create it; yet in the spirit of that America which lies hidden in some form in the aspirations of us all; in the spirit of that America for which our young men are at this moment fighting and dying; in that spirit of liberty and of America I ask you to rise and with me pledge our faith in the glorious destiny of our beloved country.

JUDGE LEARNED HAND

I AM THE FLAG

I am a composite being of all the people of America.
I am the Union if you are united.
I am one and indivisible if you are undivided.
I am as strong as the weakest link.
I am an emblem of your country.
I am a symbol of a shadow of the real.
I am a sign pointing to past achievements.
I am a promise of greater things for the future.
I am what you make me.
I am purity if you are pure.
I am bravery if you are brave.
I am loyalty if you are loyal.

I am honor if you are honorable.
I am goodness if you are good.
I am hope if you are hopeful.
I am truth if you are true.

I am the Constitution.
I am law and order.
I am tolerance or intolerance as you force me to be.
I am liberty as you understand liberty.
I am as a pillar of fire by night, but you must provide
the fuel.
I march at the head of the column, but you must
carry me on.

I stand for greater and more glorious achievement
    than can be found in recorded history, but you
    must be my inspiration.
I AM THE FLAG.

LAWRENCE M. JONES

LIBERTY AND UNION

While the Union lasts, we have high, exciting, gratifying prospects spread before us, for us and our children. Beyond that, I seek not to penetrate the veil. God grant that, in my day, at least, that curtain may not rise! God grant that on my vision never may be opened what lies behind! When my eyes shall be turned to behold for the last time the sun in heaven, may I not see him shining on the broken and dishonored fragments of a once-glorious Union; on the States dissevered, discordant, belligerent; on a land rent with civil feuds, or drenched, it may be, in fraternal blood! Let their last feeble and lingering glance rather behold the gorgeous ensign of the Republic, now known and honored throughout the earth, still full high advanced, its arms and trophics streaming in their original luster, not a stripe erased or polluted, nor a single star obscured, bearing for its motto no such miserable interrogatory as, "What is all this worth?" nor those other words of delusion and folly, "Liberty first and Union afterward"; but everywhere, spread all over in characters of living light, blazing on all its ample folds, as they float over the sea and over the land, and in every wind under the whole heavens, that other sentiment dear to every American heart — Liberty *and* Union, now and forever, one and inseparable!

DANIEL WEBSTER

From AS YOU LIKE IT

Sweet are the uses of adversity,
Which, like the toad, ugly and venomous,
Wears yet a precious jewel in his head;
And this our life exempt from public haunt
Finds tongues in trees, books in the running brooks,
Sermons in stones and good in everything.

WILLIAM SHAKESPEARE

◈◈◈

. . . A more secret, sweet, and overpowering beauty appears to man when his heart and mind open to the sentiment of virtue. Then he is instructed in what is above him. He learns that his being is without bound; that to the good, to the perfect, he is born, low as he now lies in evil and weakness. That which he venerates is still his own, though he has not realized it yet. *He ought*. He knows the sense of that grand word, though his analysis fails to render account of it. When in innocency or when by intellectual perception he attains to say, "I love the Right; Truth is beautiful within and without for evermore. Virtue, I am thine; save me; use me; thee will I serve, day and night, in great, in small . . ." then is the end of the creation answered, and God is well pleased.

RALPH WALDO EMERSON

From THE MERCHANT OF VENICE

The quality of mercy is not strained;
It droppeth as the gentle rain from heaven
Upon the place beneath: it is twice blest, —
It blesseth him that gives and him that takes:
'Tis mightiest in the mightiest; it becomes
The throned monarch better than his crown;
His sceptre shows the force of temporal power,
The attribute to awe and majesty,
Wherein doth sit the dread and fear of kings;
But mercy is above this sceptred sway, —
It is enthroned in the hearts of kings,
It is an attribute to God himself;
And earthly power doth then show likest God's,
When mercy seasons justice.

WILLIAM SHAKESPEARE

◈◈◈

The most pure democracy is that which is so called principally from that equality which prevails in it; for this is what the law in that state directs: that the poor shall be in no greater subjection than the rich; nor that the supreme power shall be lodged with either of these, but that both shall share it.

ARISTOTLE

◈◈◈

The government of a state is much like the office of a guardian or trustee, which should always be managed for the good of the pupil, and not of the persons to whom he is entrusted; and those men who, whilst they take care of one, neglect or disregard another part of the citizens do but occasion sedition and discord, the most destructive things in the world to a state.

CICERO

BROTHERHOOD

The crest and crowning of all good,
Life's final star, is Brotherhood;
For it will bring again to earth
Her long-lost Poesy and Mirth;
Will send new light on every face,
A kingly power upon the race.
And till it come, we men are slaves,
And travel downward to the dust of graves.
Come, clear the way, then, clear the way;
Blind creeds and kings have had their day;
Break the dead branches from the path;
Our hope is in the aftermath —
Our hope is in heroic men
Star-led to build the world again.
Make way for Brotherhood; make way for Man!

EDWIN MARKHAM

From ACCEPTANCE SPEECH FOR NOBEL PRIZE IN LITERATURE*

. . . I decline to accept the end of man. It is easy enough to say that man is immortal simply because he will endure: that when the last ding-dong of doom has clanged and faded from the last worthless rock hanging tideless in the last red and dying evening, that even then there will still be one more sound; that of his puny inexhaustible voice, still talking. I refuse to accept this. I believe that man will not merely endure: he will prevail. He is immortal, not because he alone among creatures has an inexhaustible voice, but because he has a soul, a spirit capable of compassion and sacrifice and endurance. The poet's, the writer's, duty is to write about these things. It is his privilege to help man endure by lifting his heart, by reminding him of the courage and honor and hope and pride and compassion and pity and sacrifice which have been the glory of his past. The poet's voice need not merely be the record of man, it can be one of the props, the pillars to help him endure and prevail.

WILLIAM FAULKNER

* Reprinted from *The Faulkner Reader*. Copyright 1954 by William Faulkner (Random House, Inc.).

DEEP WET MOSS*

Deep wet moss and cool blue shadows
Beneath a bending fir,
And the purple solitude of mountains,
When only the dark owls stir —
Oh, there will come a day, a twilight,
When I shall sink to rest
In deep wet moss and cool blue shadows
Upon a mountain's breast,
And yield a body torn with passions,
And bruised with earthly scars,
To the cool oblivion of evening,
Of solitude and stars.

LEW SARETT

The following poem was written by a 19-year-old citizen of the United States before he was killed in action with the Royal Canadian Air Force on December 11, 1941 in the vicinity of the British Isles. This poem was posted in all pilot-training centers of the British Empire during World War II. The author had a scholarship to enter Yale University, but enlisted in the R.C.A.F. instead.

HIGH FLIGHT†

Oh, I have slipped the surly bonds of earth,
And danced the skies on laughter-silvered wings;
Sunward I've climbed and joined the tumbling mirth
Of sun-split clouds — and done a hundred things
You have not dreamed of — wheeled and soared and swung
High in the sunlit silence. Hovering there,
I've chased the shouting wind along and flung
My eager craft through footless halls of air.
Up, up the long delirious, burning blue
I've topped the wind-swept heights with easy grace,
Where never lark, or even eagle, flew;
And, while with silent, lifting mind I've trod
The high untrespassed sanctity of space,
Put out my hand, and touched the face of God.

JOHN GILLESPIE MAGEE, JR.

---

* From *Covenant with Earth* by Lew Sarett. Edited and copyrighted 1956 by Alma Johnson Sarett, and published 1956 by the University of Florida Press. Reprinted by permission of Mrs. Sarett.

† By Pilot-Officer John Gillespie Magee, Jr., R.C.A.F. Reprinted by permission of the New York World Journal Tribune.

◈◈◈

Difficulties exist to be surmounted. The great heart will no more complain of the obstructions that make success hard, than of the iron walls of the gun which hinder the shot from scattering. It was walled round with iron tube with that purpose, to give it irresistible force in one direction. A strenuous soul hates cheap successes. It is the ardor of the assailant that makes the vigor of the defender. The great are not tender at being obscure, despised, insulted. Such only feel themselves in adverse fortune.

RALPH WALDO EMERSON

THE ANGRY MAN*

The other day I chanced to meet
An angry man upon the street —
A man of wrath, a man of war,
A man who truculently bore
Over his shoulder, like a lance,
A banner labeled "Tolerance."

And when I asked him why he strode
Thus scowling down the human road,
Scowling, he answered, "I am he
Who champions total liberty —
Intolerance being, ma'am, a state
No tolerant man can tolerate.

"When I meet rogues," he cried, "who choose
To cherish oppositional views,
Lady, like this, and in this manner,
I lay about me with my banner
Till they cry mercy, ma'am." His blows
Rained proudly on prospective foes.

Fearful, I turned and left him there
Still muttering, as he thrashed the air,
"Let the Intolerant beware!"

PHYLLIS MCGINLEY

OZYMANDIAS

I met a traveler from an antique land
Who said: Two vast and trunkless legs of stone
Stand in the desert. Near them, on the sand,
Half sunk, a shattered visage lies, whose frown,
And wrinkled lip, and sneer of cold command,
Tell that its sculptor well those passions read
Which yet survive, stamped on these lifeless things,
The hand that mocked them and the heart that fed;
And on the pedestal these words appear:
"My name is Ozymandias, king of kings:
Look on my works, ye Mighty, and despair!"
Nothing beside remains. Round the decay
Of that colossal wreck, boundless and bare
The lone and level sands stretch far away.

PERCY BYSSHE SHELLEY

AMERICA FIRST!*

Not merely in matters material, but in things of the spirit.
Not merely in science, inventions, motors, and skyscrapers, but also in ideals, principles, character.
Not merely in the calm assumption of rights, but in the glad assumption of duties.
Not flaunting her strength as a giant, but bending in helpfulness over a sick and wounded world like a Good Samaritan.
Not in splendid isolation, but in courageous cooperation.
Not in pride, arrogance, and disdain of other races and peoples, but in sympathy, love, and understanding.
Not in treading again the old, worn, bloody pathway which ends inevitably in chaos and disaster, but in blazing a new trail, along which, please God, other nations will follow, into the New Jerusalem where wars shall be no more.
Some day some nation must take that path — unless we are to lapse once again into utter barbarism — and that honor I covet for my beloved America.
And so, in that spirit and with these hopes, I say with all my heart and soul, "America First!"

G. ASHTON OLDHAM

* From *Patriotism, Patriotism, Patriotism* by Helen Hoke, ed. Published by Franklin Watts, Inc. Reprinted by permission of Mrs. G. Ashton Oldham.

THE LARGER AIM*

Not long ago I was disturbed to read a newspaper report of a student's speech which maintained that today's college senior views his education simply as a means toward "a better-paying job . . . more security . . . social position."

If there are students who seriously believe this, then it seems to me they have missed the main point of college — or indeed of being alive — and that we are in for trouble.

The true liberal education has larger aims than just cramming its students with facts in order to teach them how to earn a living. First, it must help each student to find himself as an individual; then it must help him to lose himself in interests, causes, and ideas larger and more enduring than he is.

America has no need for a race of young people fitted to the same pattern, content to sit back and enjoy what has been called "a prosperous conformity." But our country will always have room for imaginative, reasonable, and responsible men and women. And it desperately needs the informed and the truly creative among its young people.

I believe the teacher's mission is to help every young person in his care grow into the broadest, deepest, most vital person possible. And in fulfilling himself the student will, I am convinced, arrive at moments of heightened insight when he sees more clearly than ever before what the world is about and how he can fit into it creatively and significantly.

Viewed this way, a college education suddenly takes on new meaning — and so do the staggering estimates of college enrollment. Instead of a frightening prospect of millions of young people solely concerned with a scramble for better jobs, we can look forward confidently to a challenging tomorrow when millions of young Americans turn to college because they want to realize their full capacity as human beings, to find major pleasure in learning, to live richly and responsibly, and to do their part to help create a better world.

NATHAN M. PUSEY

◈◈◈

Let me never fall into the vulgar mistake of dreaming that I am persecuted whenever I am contradicted. No man, I think, had ever a

* From *New Treasury of Words to Live By* by William I. Nichols, ed. Copyright 1959 by Simon and Schuster, Inc. and reprinted with their permission.

greater well-being with a less desert than I. I can very well afford to be accounted bad or foolish by a few dozen or a few hundred persons — I who see myself greeted by the good expectation of so many friends far beyond any power of thought or communication of thought residing in me. Besides, I own, I am often inclined to take part with those who say I am bad or foolish, for I fear I am both. I believe and know there must be a perfect compensation. I know too well my own dark spots. Not having myself attained, not satisfied myself, far from a holy obedience — how can I expect to satisfy others, to command their love? A few sour faces, a few biting paragraphs — is but a cheap expiation for all these short-comings of mine.

RALPH WALDO EMERSON

FLOWER IN THE CRANNIED WALL

Flower in the crannied wall,
I pluck you out of the crannies,
I hold you here, root and all, in my hand,
Little flower — but *if* I could understand
What you are, root and all, and all in all,
I should know what God and man is.

ALFRED TENNYSON

◈◈◈

Life is a scale of degrees. Between rank and rank of our great men are wide intervals. Mankind have in all ages attached themselves to a few persons who either by the quality of that idea they embodied or by the largeness of their reception were entitled to the position of leaders and lawgivers. These teach us the qualities of primary nature — admit us to the constitution of things. We swim, day by day, on a river of delusions and are effectually amused with houses and towns in the air, of which the men about us are dupes. But life is a sincerity. In lucid intervals we say, "Let there be an entrance opened for me into realities; I have worn the fool's cap too long." We will know the meaning of our economies and politics. Give us the cipher, and if persons and things are scores of a celestial music, let us read off the strains. We have been cheated of our reason; yet there have been sane men, who enjoyed a rich and related existence. What they know, they know for us. With each new mind, a new secret of nature transpires; nor can the Bible be closed until the last great man is born.

RALPH WALDO EMERSON

BEAUTY*

Beauty means this to one person, perhaps, and that to the other. And yet when any one of us has seen or heard or read that which to him is beautiful, he has known an emotion which is in every case the same in kind, if not in degree; an emotion precious and uplifting. A choirboy's voice, a ship in sail, an opening flower, a town at night, the song of the blackbird, a lovely poem, leaf shadows, a child's grace, the starry skies, a cathedral, appletrees in spring, a thorough-bred horse, sheep-bells on a hill, a rippling stream, a butterfly, the crescent moon — the thousand sights or sounds or words that evoke in us the thought of beauty — these are the drops of rain that keep the human spirit from death by drought. They are a stealing and a silent refreshment that we perhaps do not think about but which goes on all the time. The war brought a kind of revolt against beauty in art, literature, and music, a revolt that is already passing, and that I am sure will pass. It would surprise any of us if we realized how much store we unconsciously set by beauty, and how little savour there would be left in life if it were withdrawn. It is the smile on the earth's face, open to all, and needs but the eyes to see, the mood to understand.

JOHN GALSWORTHY

WHOM DO I CALL EDUCATED?

Whom, then, do I call educated? First, those who control circumstances instead of being mastered by them, those who meet all occasions manfully and act in accordance with intelligent thinking, those who are honorable in all dealings, who treat good naturedly persons and things that are disagreeable, and furthermore, those who hold their pleasures under control and are not overcome by misfortune, finally those who are not spoiled by success.

ISOCRATES

◈◈◈

All writing should be selection in order to drop every dead word. Why do you not save out of your speech or thinking only the vital things — the spirited *mot* which amused or warmed you when you spoke it — because of its luck and newness? I have just been reading, in this careful book of a most intelligent and learned man, any number of flat conventional words and sentences. If a man would learn to read his own manuscript severely — becoming really a third person, and search only

* From *Candelabra* by John Galsworthy. Used by permission of Charles Scribner's Sons.

for what interested him, he would blot to purpose — and how every page would gain! Then all the words will be sprightly, and every sentence a surprise.

RALPH WALDO EMERSON

EARTH IS ENOGUH*

We men of Earth have here the stuff
Of Paradise — we have enough!
We need no other thing to build
The stairs into the Unfulfilled —
No other ivory for the doors —
No other marble for the floors —
No other cedar for the beam
And dome of man's immortal dream.
Here on the paths of everyday —
Here on the common human way
Is all the stuff the Gods would take
To build a Heaven, to mold and make
New Edens. Ours the stuff sublime
To build Eternity in Time!

EDWIN MARKHAM

KINSMEN†

A mountain pool is brother to the sky;
It mirrors every gray owl flapping by,
Holds on its silver all the traceries
Of clouds and overarching trees.

The wash of water and of wind is one;
And any lapsing pond gives back the sun,
Doubles the ragged scarlet in the west,
And holds the stars upon its breast.

Even as tranquil water in a hollow
Mirrors the fleeting shadow of a swallow,
Oh, even so am I content to be
Kinsman of sky and wind and sea.

LEW SARETT

* Reprinted by permission of Virgil Markham.
† From *Covenant with Earth* by Lew Sarett. Edited and copyrighted 1956 by Alma Johnson Sarett, and published 1956 by the University of Florida Press. Reprinted by permission of Mrs. Sarett.

There is no history. There is only biography. The attempt to perpetrate, to fix a thought or principle, fails continually. You can only live for yourself; your action is good only whilst it is alive — whilst it is in you. The awkward imitation of it by your child or your disciple is not a repetition of it, is not the same thing, but another thing. The new individual must work out the whole problem of science, letters and theology for himself; can owe his fathers nothing. There is no history; only biography.

RALPH WALDO EMERSON

From RENASCENCE*

The world stands out on either side
No wider than the heart is wide;
Above the world is stretched the sky, —
No higher than the soul is high.
The heart can push the sea and land
Farther away on either hand;
The soul can split the sky in two,
And let the face of God shine through.
But East and West will pinch the heart
That cannot keep them pushed apart;
And he whose soul is flat — the sky
Will cave in on him by and by.

EDNA ST. VINCENT MILLAY

TO SEE A WORLD

To see a world in a grain of sand
And a heaven in a wild flower,
Hold Infinity in the palm of your hand
And Eternity in an hour.

WILLIAM BLAKE

◈◈◈

The "six mistakes of man" are:

The delusion that individual advancement is made by crushing others.

The tendency to worry about things that cannot be changed or corrected.

---

* From *Collected Poems,* Harper and Row. Copyright 1912, 1940 by Edna St. Vincent Millay. Permission of Norma Millay Ellis.

Insisting that a thing is impossible because we cannot accomplish it.

Refusing to set aside trivial preferences.

Neglecting development and refinement of the mind, and not acquiring the habit of reading and study.

Attempting to compel other persons to believe and live as we do.

CICERO

ACCEPTANCE*

When the spent sun throws up its rays on cloud
And goes down burning into the gulf below,
No voice in nature is heard to cry aloud
At what has happened. Birds, at least, must know
It is the change to darkness in the sky.
Murmuring something quiet in its breast,
One bird begins to close a faded eye;
Or overtaken too far from its nest
Hurrying low above the grove, some waif
Swoops just in time to his remembered tree.
At most he thinks or twitters softly, "Safe!
Now let the night be too dark for me to see
Into the future. Let what will be be."

ROBERT FROST

ARISE! ARISE!†

Though the stars riot and the heavens fall
And the least wind provokes a gathering chill,
How can the living dead remain so still
When every morning is a bugle call.

Since the free spirit turns against despair
Arise! Arise! Summon all strength and skill.
Never accept the cowardly come-what-will;
We were not born to dally, but to dare.

* From *Complete Poems of Robert Frost*. Copyright 1916, 1923, 1928 by Holt, Rinehart and Winston, Inc. Copyright 1944, 1951, © 1956 by Robert Frost. Reprinted by permission of Holt, Rinehart and Winston, Inc.

† From *Stars to Steer By*, edited by Louis Untermeyer, copyright, 1941, by Harcourt, Brace and World, Inc. and reprinted with their permission.

Who can lie listlessly in ivory towers!
Are we not given courage to engage
The evil nightmare of unspeakable powers
And storm indifference with a joyful rage?
Armed with a purpose and this dream of ours,
Arise! Arise! Confront this challenging age.

LOUIS UNTERMEYER

◈◈◈

Loaves of bread . . . honey in the honeycomb . . . summer haystacks . . . the flames of candles . . . the flight of birds . . . the darting of schools of fish . . . the shadows of clouds . . . the rising and sinking of the sun . . . old buildings, old rituals, old mythologies . . . the annual procession of the seasons . . . weeds and shells at the ocean's edge, wet pebbles and the thin black windrow . . . rain on roofs . . . thunder on horizons . . . murmuring of brooks, sweetness of grass . . . sadness of stirred leaves . . . the deep symbolic meaning of such objects as a plough, a sword, a grindstone, a windmill, a boat, a cradle, a coffin . . . the friendliness of wind-tossed smoke, arising from hearth or chimney . . . the forlornness of swaying reed-tops above lonely salt-marshes . . . the warmth of sun-scented leaf-mould . . . the horns of goats, the spouting of whales . . . frost marks in ditch-mud . . . vapour-circles around misty moons . . . rivers and highways that carry old legends, old memories, old tragic transactions into the unborn future — all these things, and the emanations proceeding from these things, possess some mysterious quality in common; and it would seem that this quality cannot be named by any other name than that of *the poetical element* in life.*

JOHN COWPER POWYS

THE MASTER

A flying word from here and there
Had sown the name at which we sneered,
But soon the name was everywhere,
To be reviled and then revered:
A presence to be loved and feared,
We cannot hide it, or deny
That we, the gentlemen who jeered,
May be forgotten by and by.

---

* From *The Meaning of Culture* by John Cowper Powys. Reprinted by permission of W. W. Norton and Company, Inc. Copyright 1929, 1939, by W. W. Norton & Company, Inc.; Copyright renewed 1957 by John Cowper Powys.

He came when days were perilous
And hearts of men were sore beguiled;
And having made his note of us,
He pondered and was reconciled.
Was ever master yet so mild
As he, and so untamable?
We doubted, even when he smiled,
Not knowing what he knew so well.

He knew that undeceiving fate
Would shame us whom he served unsought;
He knew that he must wince and wait —
The jest of those for whom he fought;
He knew devoutly what he thought
Of us and of our ridicule;
He knew that we must all be taught
Like little children in a school.

We gave a glamour to the task
That he encountered and saw through,
But little of us did he ask,
And little did we ever do.
And what appears if we review
The season when we railed and chaffed?
It is the face of one who knew
That we were learning while we laughed.

The face that in our vision feels
Again the venom that we flung,
Transfigured to the world reveals
The vigilance to which we clung.
Shrewd, hallowed, harassed, and among
The mysteries that are untold,
The face we see was never young
Nor could it wholly have been old.

For he, to whom we had applied
Our shopman's test of age and worth,
Was elemental when he died,
As he was ancient at his birth:
The saddest among kings of earth,
Bowed with a galling crown, this man
Met rancor with a cryptic mirth,
Laconic — and Olympian.

The love, the grandeur, and the fame
Are bounded by the world alone;
The calm, the smouldering, and the flame
Of awful patience were his own:
With him they are forever flown
Past all our fond self-shadowings,
Wherewith we cumber the Unknown
As with inept, Icarian wings.

For we were not as other men:
'Twas ours to soar and his to see;
But we are coming down again,
And we shall come down pleasantly;
Nor shall we longer disagree
On what it is to be sublime,
But flourish in our perigee
And have one Titan at a time.

EDWIN ARLINGTON ROBINSON

◈◈◈

A heavy darkness had come inside the cabin. Passengers were indistinct shapes, kneeling at the windows — to absorb the spell of the hour. The remnants of the sun streaked the cloud banked horizon ahead, making it vividly red and savagely beautiful. We were high, and the motors throbbed in a timeless rhythm. Below us were the green peaks of the Atlas Mountains, lovely in the softening shroud of the dusk. Villages with red roofs nested on the peaktops. Down below lived sheep men — obscure mountain men who had never heard of a Nebelwerfer or a bazooka, men at home at the end of the day in the poor, narrow, beautiful security of their own walls.

And there high in the sky above us and yet a part of it all were plain Americans incongruously away from home. For a moment it seemed terribly dramatic that we should be there at all amid that darkening beauty so far away, so foreign, and so old.

It was one of those moments impossible to transmit to another mind. A moment of overpowering beauty, of the surge of a marching world, of the relentlessness of our own fate. It made me want to cry.*

ERNIE PYLE

---

* From *Brave Men* by Ernie Pyle. Copyright 1943, 1944 by Scripps-Howard Newspaper Alliance. Copyright 1944 by Holt, Rinehart and Winston, Inc. Reprinted by permission of Holt, Rinehart and Winston, Inc.

From TRISTRAM*

I am not one
Who must have everything; yet I must have
My dreams if I must live, for they are mine.
Wisdom is not one word and then another,
Till words are like dry leaves under a tree;
Wisdom is like a dawn that comes up slowly
Out of an unknown ocean.

Edwin Arlington Robinson

COURAGE†

Courage is the price that life exacts for granting peace.
The soul that knows it not, knows no release
From little things;

Knows not the livid loneliness of fear
Nor mountain heights, where bitter joy can hear
The sound of wings.

How can life grant us boon of living, compensate
For dull gray ugliness and pregnant hate
Unless we dare

The soul's dominion? Each time we make a choice, we pay
With courage to behold resistless day
And count it fair.

Amelia Earhart

From OTHELLO

Good name in man and woman, dear my lord,
Is the immediate jewel of their souls:
Who steals my purse steals trash; 'tis something, nothing;
'Twas mine, 'tis his, and has been slave to thousands;
But he that filches from me my good name
Robs me of that which not enriches him,
And makes me poor indeed.

William Shakespeare

LINCOLN, THE MAN OF THE PEOPLE

When the Norn Mother saw the Whirlwind Hour
Greatening and darkening as it hurried on,
She left the Heaven of Heroes and came down
To make a man to meet the mortal need.
She took the tried clay of the common road —
Clay warm yet with the genial heat of Earth,
Dashed through it all a strain of prophecy;
Tempered the heap with thrill of human tears;
Then mixed a laughter with the serious stuff.
Into the shape she breathed a flame to light
That tender, tragic, ever-changing face.
Here was a man to hold against the world,
A man to match the mountains and the sea.

The color of the ground was in him, the red earth;
The smell and smack of elemental things:
The rectitude and patience of the cliff;
The good-will of the rain that loves all leaves;
The friendly welcome of the wayside well;
The courage of the bird that dares the sea;
The gladness of the wind that shakes the corn;
The pity of the snow that hides all scars;
The secrecy of streams that make their way
Beneath the mountain to the rifted rock;
The tolerance and equity of light
That gives as freely to the shrinking flower
As to the great oak flaring to the wind —
To the grave's low hill as to the Matterhorn
That shoulders out the sky.

Sprung from the West,
The strength of virgin forests braced his mind,
The hush of spacious prairies stilled his soul.
Up from log cabin to the Capitol,
One fire was on his spirit, one resolve —
To send the keen ax to the root of wrong,
Clearing a free way for the feet of God.
And evermore he burned to do his deed
With the fine stroke and gesture of a king:
He built the rail-pile as he built the State,
Pouring his splendid strength through every blow,
The conscience of him testing every stroke.
To make his deed the measure of a man.

So came the Captain with the mighty heart;
And when the judgment thunders split the house,
Wrenching the rafters from their ancient rest,
He held the ridgepole up, and spiked again
The rafters of the Home. He held his place —
Held the long purpose like a growing tree —
Held on through blame and faltered not at praise.
And when he fell in whirlwind, he went down
As when a lordly cedar, green with boughs,
Goes down with a great shout upon the hills,
And leaves a lonesome place against the sky.

EDWIN MARKHAM

A PASSAGE TO INDIA

I see over my own continent the Pacific railroad surmounting
every barrier,
I see continual trains of cars winding along the Platte carrying
freight and passengers,
I hear the locomotives rushing and roaring, and the shrill
steam-whistle,
I hear the echoes reverberate through the grandest scenery in
the world,
I cross the Laramie plains, I note the rocks in grotesque
shapes, the buttes,
I see the plentiful larkspur and wild onions, the barren,
colorless, sage-deserts,
I see in glimpses afar or towering immediately above me the
great mountains, I see the Wind river and the Wahsatch
mountains,
I see the Monument mountain and the Eagle's Nest, I pass the
Promontory, I ascend the Nevadas,
I scan the noble Elk mountain and wind around its base,
I see the Humboldt range, I thread the valley and cross the
river.
I see the clear waters of lake Tahoe, I see forests of majestic
pines,
Or crossing the great desert, the alkaline plains, I behold
enchanting mirages of waters and meadows,
Marking through these and after all, in duplicate slender lines,
Bridging the three or four thousand miles of land travel,
Tying the Eastern to the Western sea,
The road between Europe and Asia.

WALT WHITMAN

BROTHERHOOD—BELIEVE IT, LIVE IT, SUPPORT IT*

BROTHERHOOD — BELIEVE IT!

Defined as a willingness to give to others every right and dignity we claim for ourselves, brotherhood is essential to the fulfillment and perpetuation of American democracy. Until that conviction controls the thinking of our citizens, democracy is not safe. So long as any minority among us is not free, all of us are threatened. That belief is fundamental.

BROTHERHOOD — LIVE IT!

That injunction finds us where we dwell. It reaches into our schools, our churches, our community organizations. Every denial of brotherhood anywhere menaces its establishment everywhere. It is our contention that the world-wide acceptance of brotherhood as the rule of life for nations is essential to permanent peace . . . What we do in our own country speaks more loudly to the world than anything we can say.

BROTHERHOOD — SUPPORT IT!

That is, spread brotherhood. It is necessary, but not sufficient, to believe brotherhood and to live it as persons and citizens. We must proclaim it, be its advocates. Brotherhood has many adversaries. Selfishness, prejudice, ignorance, are divisive. They disrupt the human family, drive and hold its members apart. We must educate for brotherhood in every community in the land. We must establish conditions within which brotherhood is possible. The friends of brotherhood must seek each other out and put their heads together. We must campaign for brotherhood. For the fight for brotherhood is never completely won. There is no surcease to this war. Strategy and tactics must be adapted to conditions as we find and face them. All of us — together!

THE NATIONAL CONFERENCE OF CHRISTIANS AND JEWS

THE CITIZEN'S RESPONSIBILITY

. . . To fight for one's country when its life is threatened by violence is noble and heroic; to stand up for it in peace time is a virtue quite as

* Used by permission of The National Conference of Christians and Jews, Inc.

necessary. And unless there be such virtue in citizenship, our traditions will be forgotten, our ideals neglected and our institutions will crumble.

What is more important to every citizen of this Republic than the perpetuity of the institutions which protect his life, his liberty and his property; what is of more priceless value than the national ideals and traditions which have given this nation its proud place in history? Yet how little thought the average man or woman gives to this most vital of all questions affecting the most precious things in life!

Institutions, governments, do not preserve themselves. They can be preserved only by the vigilance of those to whose guardianship they have been committed. Upon you, as a citizen of the Republic, rests a responsibility which cannot be shirked without danger to your country. Its future is worth something of your thought, so much of which is given to matters of less moment.

From THE NATIONAL REPUBLIC

◈◈◈

One must not cut oneself off from the world. No one who lives in the sunlight makes a failure of his life. My whole effort, whatever the situation, misfortune or disillusion, must be to make contact again. But even within this sadness I feel a great leap of joy and a great desire to love simply at the sight of a hill against the evening sky.*

ALBERT CAMUS

THOUGHTS FOR THE DAY

Arranged by Groups in Ascending Order of Difficulty

Brief excerpts from preceding material have been repeated in this section whenever it seemed desirable

THOUGHTS FOR THE DAY

Easy to Understand

Arranged alphabetically by first word except for A, An *and* The.

Actions speak louder than words. — *Anonymous*

Be always merry as ever you can,
For no one delights in a sorrowful man. — *Anonymous*

Be as polite to your parents, brothers, and sisters as you are to strangers. — *Anonymous*

Be ashamed to catch yourself idle. — FRANKLIN

Be good, do good, and you will be happy. — *Anonymous*

Be quick to forgive and slow to anger. — *Anonymous*

The beginning is the most important part of the work. — PLATO

Better do a little well than a great deal badly. — SOCRATES

Blessed is the man that has found his work. — CARLYLE

A child should always say what's true
And speak when he is spoken to
And behave mannerly at table
At least as far as he is able. — STEVENSON

"Don't cross the bridge till you come to it."
Is a proverb old, and of excellent wit. — LONGFELLOW

Duty before pleasure. — *Anonymous*

Everyone who does the best he can is a hero. — BILLINGS

Except a living man, there is nothing more wonderful than a book. — *Anonymous*

A friend in need is a friend indeed. — *Anonymous*

Good manners and soft words have brought many a difficult thing to pass. — AESOP

Good manners cannot be put on at pleasure, like an outside coat, but must belong to us. *Anonymous*

Good manners may in seven words be found:
Forget yourself and think of those around. GUITERMAN

A good name is rather to be chosen than great riches. *Holy Bible*

Govern thyself and thou will be able to govern the world. *Chinese Proverb*

Haste makes waste. HEYWOOD

He can who believes he can. *Latin Proverb*

He enjoys much who is thankful for little. SECKER

He that does good to another does good to himself. SENECA

He who sows courtesy reaps friendship, and he who plants kindness gathers love. *Anonymous*

Hearts, like doors, will ope with ease
To very, very little keys;
And don't forget that two of these
Are "Thank you, sir," and "If you please." *Nursery Rhyme*

Honesty is the best policy. *Anonymous*

Honor thy father and thy mother. *Holy Bible*

I had six honest serving men. They taught me all I knew: Their names were Where and What and When and Why and How and Who. KIPLING

If a task is once begun,
Do not leave it till it's done. *Anonymous*

If a first you don't succeed, try, try again. HICKSON

If we do not watch, we lose our opportunities. SENECA

If you want to sing, you will find a song. *Anonymous*

It is good to be unselfish and generous. ELIOT

It is more blessed to give than to receive. *Holy Bible*

Just a little every day;
That's the way
Children learn to read and write,
Bit by bit and mite by mite.
Never any one, I say,
Leaps to knowledge and its power.
Slowly, slowly — hour by hour —
That's the way;
Just a little every day. WILCOX

Kind words are little sunbeams,
That sparkle as they fall;
And loving smiles are sunbeams,
A light of joy to all. *Anonymous*

Life is not so short but that there is always time enough for courtesy. EMERSON

Make hay while the sun shines. *Anonymous*

One good turn deserves another. BEAUMONT & FLETCHER

The only way to have a friend is to be one. EMERSON

A penny saved is a penny got. STEELE

A place for everything, everything in its place. FRANKLIN

Politeness is to do and say
The kindest thing in the kindest way. *Anonymous*

Refuse to do a mean act, be it ever so small. *Anonymous*

Slow and steady wins the race. AESOP

So here hath been dawning
Another blue Day:
Think, wilt thou let it
Slip useless away? CARLYLE

Something is learned every time a book is opened. *Chinese Proverb*

Step by step one goes far. *Italian Proverb*

There is only one rule for being a good talker;
learn how to listen. — MORLEY

There's a time for some things
and a time for all things;
a time for great things,
and a time for small things. — CERVANTES

They think too little who talk too much. — DRYDEN

To be happy you must forget yourself. — BULWER-LYTTON

To have the harvest, we must sow the seed. — BAILEY

True happiness is found in making others happy. — *Anonymous*

True worth is in *being*, not *seeming;*
In doing, each day that goes by,
Some little good — not in dreaming
Of great things to do by and by. — CARY

We can do anything we want to do if we stick to it long enough. — KELLER

When you play, play hard, but when you work, don't play at all. — ROOSEVELT

A willing helper does not wait until he is asked. — *Danish Proverb*

A wise old owl lived in an oak;
The more he heard the less he spoke;
The less he spoke the more he heard:
Why can't we all be like that bird? — *Anonymous*

Work while you work, play while you play;
This is the way to be cheerful and gay.
All that you do, do with your might;
Things done by halves are never done right. — STODART

The world is so full of a number of things,
I'm sure we should all be as happy as kings. — STEVENSON

You have never seen a happy face ugly. — LOCKE

THOUGHTS FOR THE DAY

Needing Some Reflection

Arranged alphabetically by first word except for A, An *and* The.

After a bad harvest, sow again. — *Latin Proverb*

All things are easy to industry,
All things are difficult to sloth. — FRANKLIN

The Americans have what every man worthy of the name of man must have — a country to live for; if need be, a country to die for. — CARNEGIE

Arguing is a game that two can play at, but it is a strange game in that neither opponent ever wins. — FRANKLIN

As a moth gnaws a garment, so doth envy consume a man. — ST. CHRYSOSTOM

The badge of honesty is simplicity. — NOVALIS

Be not merely good; be good for something. — THOREAU

Be slow of tongue and quick of eye. — CERVANTES

Behave toward every one as if receiving a great guest. — CONFUCIUS

The best way to keep good acts in memory is to refresh them with new. — CATO

Better little talent and much purpose than much talent and little purpose. — *Anonymous*

Birds of a feather will flock together. — MINSHEU

Books are keys to wisdom's treasure;
Books are gates to lands of pleasure;
Books are paths that upward lead;
Books are friends. Come, let us read. — POULSSON

By all these lovely tokens
September days are here,
With summer's best of weather
And autumn's best of cheer. — JACKSON

Carelessness does more harm than a want of knowledge. — FRANKLIN

Cheerful company shortens the miles. — *German Proverb*

Cleanliness is next to godliness. — WESLEY

Difficulties strengthen the mind as labor does the body. — SENECA

The difficulty in life is the choice. — MOORE

Do all the good you can,
By all the means you can,
In all the ways you can,
In all the places you can,
At all the times you can,
To all the people you can,
As long as ever you can. — WESLEY

Do not speak of your happiness to one less fortunate than yourself. — PLUTARCH

Do the duty that is best,
Leave unto the Lord the rest. — LONGFELLOW

Do the duty which lies nearest to thee. — GOETHE

Do what you ought, come what may. — *French Proverb*

Don't talk about what you have done or what you are going to do — do it and let it speak for itsel. — VANBEE

Early to bed and early to rise,
Makes a man healthy, wealthy, and wise. — FRANKLIN

Every one excels in something in which another fails. — SYRUS

Faithfulness in little things fits one for heroism when the great trials come. — ALCOTT

Fight thine own faults, not the faults of others. — CONFUCIUS

The first step to greatness is to be honest. — JOHNSON

For every evil under the sun,
There is a remedy or there is none;
If there be one, try and find it;
If there be none, never mind it. — *Old English Rhyme*

Forewarned is forearmed. — *Anonymous*

The fountain of wisdom flows through books. — *Greek Proverb*

A friend must not be injured, even in jest. — SYRUS

Friends, if we be honest with ourselves, we shall be honest with each other. — MACDONALD

A friendship is a precious thing, too precious to destroy
A hasty word can spoil it all, and crush life's greatest joy. — CLARKE

Friendship is the most pleasant of all things, and nothing more gladdens the heart of man. — PLUTARCH

Friendship multiplies joys and divides griefs. — *Anonymous*

From the errors of others, a wise man corrects his own. — SYRUS

Glass, china and reputation are easily cracked and never well mended. — FRANKLIN

Gold helps those who help themselves. — SIDNEY

A good book is the best of friends, the same today and forever. — TUPPER

A good conscience is a continual Christmas. — FRANKLIN

A good laugh is sunshine in a house. — THACKERAY

A grateful mind is a great mind. — SECKER

The greater the obstacle, the more glory in overcoming it. — MOLIERE

Habit is a cable; we weave a thread of it every day, and at last we cannot break it. — MANN

The happiest person is the person who thinks the most interesting thoughts. — DWIGHT

Happy hearts and happy faces,
Happy play in grassy places,
That was how, in ancient ages,
Children grew to kings and sages. — STEVENSON

Happy is the man that findeth wisdom, and the man that getteth understanding . . . — *Holy Bible*

Have you had a kindness shown? Pass it on. — BURTON

He that goes a-borrowing goes a-sorrowing. — FRANKLIN

He that riseth late must trot all day. — FRANKLIN

He that would have the fruit must climb the tree. — *Anonymous*

He that would live in peace and at ease, must not speak all he knows, nor judge all he sees. — FRANKLIN

He who is afraid of doing too much always does too little. — *German Proverb*

He who is noble performs noble deeds. — *Dutch Proverb*

He who serves many masters must neglect some. — *Spanish Proverb*

He who sings frightens away his ills. — CERVANTES

He who wants little always has enough. — ZIMMERMAN

Heroism consists in hanging on one minute longer. — *Norwegian Proverb*

Hide not your talents, they for use were made.
What's a sun-dial in the shade? — FRANKLIN

Honesty in little things is not a little thing. — *Anonymous*

I don't think much of a man who is not wiser today than he was yesterday. — LINCOLN

I fear nothing but doing wrong. — STERNE

I leave this rule for others when I'm dead,
Be always sure you're right — then go ahead. CROCKETT

I realize that patriotism is not enough. I must have no hatred toward any one. CAVELL

If a man empties his purse into his head, no man can take it away from him. An investment in knowledge always pays the best interest. FRANKLIN

If a man would be brave, let him obey his conscience. CLARKE

If you would reap praise you must sow the seeds, gentle words and useful deeds. FRANKLIN

Ignore dull days; forget the showers;
Keep count of only shining hours. UNTERMEYER

I'll study and get ready, and be prepared for my opportunity when it comes LINCOLN

It is better to learn late than never. SYRUS

It is hard to fail, but it is worse never to have tried to succeed. ROOSEVELT

It is what we do that counts, not what we intend to do. *Anonymous*

Keep conscience clear, then never fear. FRANKLIN

A kind word is never thrown away. *Anonymous*

Kindness is a language the deaf can hear and the dumb can understand. BOVEE

Knowledge, like everything else of the highest value, is not to be obtained easily. ARNOLD

Laugh, and the world laughs with you;
Weep, and you weep alone
For the sad old earth must borrow its mirth,
But has trouble enough of its own. WILCOX

Let me be a little kinder
Let me be a little blinder
To the faults of those around me
Let me praise a little more. GUEST

Let not thyself be easily angered. ELIEZER

Let thy speech be better than silence or be silent. DIONYSIUS THE ELDER

Light is the task when many share the toil. HOMER

Little strokes fell great oaks. FRANKLIN

Live to learn and you will learn to live. *Portuguese Proverb*

Look before, or you'll find yourself behind. FRANKLIN

Look before you leap. HEYWOOD

Lost time is never found again. FRANKLIN

Lost, yesterday, somewhere between sunrise and sunset, two golden hours, each set with sixty diamond minutes.
No reward is offered for they are gone forever. MANN

The man who can't make a mistake can't make anything. LINCOLN

Manners are the happy way of doing things. EMERSON

Maybe you cannot always be best,
But you can always be better. SARTON

Men are great only as they are considerate and kind. *Anonymous*

Never leave that till tomorrow which you can do today. FRANKLIN

Never trouble another with what you can do yourself. JEFFERSON

No man is free who cannot command himself. EPICTETUS

No one can disgrace us but ourselves. HOLLAND

No one can harm you except yourself. GOETHE

No one knows what he can do till he tries. SYRUS

No Quarrel ever Stirred
Before the Second Word. GUITERMAN

No really great man ever thought himself so. HAZLITT

Not failure, but low aim, is crime. LOWELL

Not what we give, but what we share,
For the gift without the giver is bare.
Who gives himself with his alms feeds three
Himself, his hungering neighbor, and Me. LOWELL

Not what you Get, but what you Give
Is that which proves your Right to Live. GUITERMAN

Nothing is so hard, but search will find it out. HERRICK

Nothing ventured, nothing gained. HEYWOOD

An oak is not felled at one blow. *Spanish Proverb*

Obedience is our universal duty and destiny. CARLYLE

One today is worth two tomorrows. FRANKLIN

Only the educated are free. EPICTETUS

Opportunity knocks but once. *Anonymous*

Patience is power; with time and patience the mulberry leaf becomes silk. *Chinese Proverb*

People often grudge others what they cannot enjoy themselves. AESOP

The person who really thinks learns quite as much from his failures as from his successes. DEWEY

Politeness is real kindness kindly expressed. WITHERSPOON

Quarrels never could last long
If on one side were all the wrong. FRANKLIN

Receive all men with cheerfulness. SHAMMAI

The reward of a thing well done is to have done it. EMERSON

The secret of happiness is something to do. BURROUGHS

Silence is golden. WHITE

A slip of the foot you may soon recover, but a slip of the tongue you may never get over. FRANKLIN

A soft answer turneth away wrath:
But grievous words stir up anger. *Holy Bible*

Sow an act and you reap a habit. Sow a habit and you reap a character. Sow a character and you reap a destiny. READE

Speak not but what may benefit others or yourself. FRANKLIN

A stitch in time saves nine. *Anonymous*

The stormy March has come at last
With wind, and cloud, and changing skies;
I hear the rushing of the blast
That through the snowy valley flies. BRYANT

Strike while the iron is hot. SCOTT

Success does not consist in never making blunders, but in never making the same one the second time. SHAW

Success is getting what you want; happiness is wanting what you get. *Anonymous*

The sweetest of all sounds is praise. XENOPHON

There is always a best way of doing everything, if it be to boil an egg. EMERSON

Therefore all things whatsoever ye would that men should do to you, do ye even so to them: for this is the law and the prophets. *Holy Bible*

There's none so blind as they that won't see. SWIFT

They conquer who believe they can. VIRGIL

Think that day lost, whose low descending sun,
Views from thy hand no worthy action done. *Anonymous*

Think the truth, speak the truth, act the truth. *Anonymous*

Thinking well is wise; planning well, wiser; doing well, wisest and best of all. *Persian Proverb*

A thousand probabilities do not make one truth. *Italian Proverb*

Time and tide wait for no man. CHAUCER

'Tis not what we have, but what we enjoy that makes us happy. *Anonymous*

To be humble when you are praised is a great and rare attainment. ST. BERNARD

To do two things at once is to do neither. SYRUS

To give — and forgive —
Is a good way to live. UNTERMEYER

Trifles make perfection, and perfection is no trifle. MICHELANGELO

True bravery is quiet, undemonstrative. SIDNEY

True courage dares to do right. *Anonymous*

True courage is to do without witnesses everything that one is capable of doing before all the world. LA ROCHEFOUCAULD

True friendship is a plant of slow growth. WASHINGTON

True politeness consists in treating others just as you love to be treated yourself. CHESTERFIELD

Trust thyself only, and another shall not betray thee. *Anonymous*

Truth is better than gold. *Arabian Proverb*

Two heads are better than one. HEYWOOD

Unfaithfulness in the keeping of an appointment is an act of clear dishonesty. You may as well borrow a person's money as his time. MANN

An unkind word falls easily from the tongue, but a coach with six horses cannot bring at back. *Chinese Proverb*

Use today wisely and your tomorrow will serve you well. PATRI

The way to be nothing is to do nothing. HOWE

The way to take a journey of a thousand miles is to take the first step. *Chinese Proverb*

What makes life worth the living
Is our giving and forgiving. SPRINGER

What a fool does in the end, the wise man does in the beginning. *Spanish Proverb*

What cannot be cured must be endured. *Latin Proverb*

Whatever is worth doing at all is worth doing well. CHESTERFIELD

Whatever work comes to your hand,
Do your best with right good will. *Anonymous*

What's done can't be undone. SHAKESPEARE

Whatsoever things are true,
Whatsoever things are honest,
Whatsoever things are just,
Whatsoever things are pure,
Whatsoever things are lovely,
Whatsoever things are of good report;
If there be any virtue,
And if there be any praise,
Think on these things. *Holy Bible*

When a man undertakes to do his work himself, it is not likely that he will be disappointed. AESOP

When angry, count to ten before you speak; if very angry, a hundred. — JEFFERSON

When the horse has been stolen, the fool shuts the stable. — *French Proverb*

When you have a lemon, make a lemonade. — ROSENWALD

When you're good to others, you are best to yourself. — FRANKLIN

Where Liberty dwells, there is my country. — FRANKLIN

Wherever there is a human being there is a chance for kindness. — SENECA

Wherever you're going, begin where you are. — NEHRU

Who bravely dares must sometimes risk a fall. — SMOLLETT

The wise make tools of whatever comes to hand. — *Anonymous*

With perseverance one surmounts all difficulties. — *Greek Proverb*

Without faith a man can do nothing. — AMIEL

A word to the wise is sufficient. — *Latin Proverb*

A work well begun is half ended. — PLATO

You measure every man's honesty by your own. — *Anonymous*

You yourself must set flame to the faggots which you have brought. — *Goodman Theater Art Institute of Chicago*

THOUGHTS FOR THE DAY

Requiring Considerable Thoughtfulness

Arranged alphabetically by first word except for A, An *and* The.

America is a tune. It must be sung together. — LEE

And now abideth faith, hope, love, these three;
but the greatest of these is love. — *Holy Bible*

Another man's burden is always light. — *Danish Proverb*

Any man may commit a mistake, but none but
a fool will continue it. — CICERO

Any one can hold the helm when the sea is calm. — SYRUS

April cold with dropping rain
Willows and lilacs bring again,
The whistle of returning birds
And trumpet-lowing of the herds. — EMERSON

Ask they purse what thou shouldst buy. — *Scotch Proverb*

Beauty lives with kindness. — SHAKESPEARE

Behavior is a mirror in which everyone shows
his image. — GOETHE

The best preparation for the future is the
present well seen to, the last duty well done. — MACDONALD

The best way out of a difficulty is through it. — *Anonymous*

Better an empty purse than an empty head. — *Anonymous*

Books are the sole means of communication with great minds of the past, and the only means most of us have to commune with the first-rate minds of our own day. In our books are recorded all the thoughts, feelings, passions, visions, and dreams that have stirred the human mind. — *Anonymous*

Character is built out of circumstances. From exactly the same material, one man builds palaces, while another man builds hovels. — LEWIS

Character is like a tree and reputation like its shadow. The shadow is what we think of it; the tree is the real thing. LINCOLN

Character is much easier kept than recovered. PAINE

Charity begins at home yet should not end there. *Greek Proverb*

Democracy is based upon the conviction that there are extraordinary possibilities in ordinary people. FOSDICK

Diligence is the mother of good luck. FRANKLIN

Doing an injury puts you below your enemy;
Revenging one makes you but even with him;
Forgiving it sets you above him. FRANKLIN

Dost thou love life? Then do not squander time; for that's the stuff life is made of. FRANKLIN

Drudgery is as necessary to call out the treasures of the mind as harrowing and planting those of the earth. FULLER

Duty is carrying on promptly and faithfully the affairs now before you. GOETHE

Education is simply the encouragement of right habits — the fixing of good habits until they become part of one's nature, and are exercised automatically. HUBBARD

Every great and commanding movement in the annals of the world is the triumph of enthusiasm. EMERSON

Everything has its beauty, but not everyone sees it. CONFUCIUS

Excellence is never granted to man, but as a reward of labor. REYNOLDS

Experience keeps a dear school, but fools will learn in no other, and scarce in that. FRANKLIN

Few persons have courage enough to appear as good as they really are. HARE

Few things are impossible to diligence and skill. JOHNSON

For without belitlting the courage with which men have died, we should not forget those acts of courage with which men . . . have lived. The courage of life is often a less dramatic spectacle than the courage of a final moment; but it is no less a magnificent mixture of triumph and tragedy. KENNEDY

Forgiveness is better than revenge. PITTACUS

A forgiveness ought to be like a cancelled note, torn in two and burned up, so that it never can be shown against the man. BEECHER

Fortune can take away riches, but not courage. SENECA

Freedom is not the right to do as one pleases but the opportunity to please to do what is right. MARSHALL

A friend is a person with whom I may be sincere.
Before him, I may think aloud. EMERSON

The friends thou hast and their adoption tried,
grapple them to thy soul with hoops of steel. SHAKESPEARE

From a little spark may burst a mighty flame. DANTE

Gather ye rosebuds while ye may,
Old time is still a-flying;
And this same flower that smiles today,
Tomorrow will be dying. HERRICK

Genius is the capacity for taking infinte pains. CARLYLE

Give us serenity to accept what cannot be changed, courage to change what should be changed and wisdom to know one from the other. *Anonymous*

Good manners are made up of petty sacrifices. EMERSON

Great minds must be ready not only to take opportunities, but to make them. COLTON

The great secret of happiness is to be at ease with yourself. — FONTENELLE

The great secret of success in life is to be ready when your opportunity comes. — DISRAELI

The great thing in the world is not so much where we stand, as in what direction we are moving. — HOLMES

Greater is he who conquers himself than he who conquers a thousand. — BUDDHA

The greatest remedy for anger is delay. — SENECA

The greatest truths are commonly the simplest. — MALESHERBES

Happiness is in the taste, and not in the things themselves. It is by having what we like that we are made happy, not by having what others think desirable. — LA ROCHEFOUCAULD

He has not learned the lesson of life who does not every day surmount a fear. — EMERSON

He that can have patience can have what he will. — FRANKLIN

He that composes himself is wiser than he that composes books. — FRANKLIN

He that respects himself is safe from others;
He wears a coat of armor that none can pierce. — LONGFELLOW

He that spares the wicked injures the good. — SYRUS

Hitch your wagon to a star. — EMERSON

An honest heart possesses a kingdom. — SENECA

Honesty needs no disguise or ornament. — OTWAY

A house without books is like a room without windows. — MANN

I am not bound to win but I am bound to be true. I am not bound to succeed but I am bound to live up to what light I have. I must stand with anybody that stands right: stand with him while he is right and part with him when he goes wrong. LINCOLN

I am only one
But still I *am* one.
I cannot do everything,
But still I can do something;
And because I cannot do everything,
I will not refuse to do the something
I can do HALE

I do the very best I know how — the very best I can; and I mean to keep doing so until the end. LINCOLN

I know not what course others may take; but as for me, give me liberty, or give me death! HENRY

I only regret that I have but one life to lose for my country. HALE

If a man can write a better book, preach a better sermon, or make a better mouse-trap than his neighbor, though he builds his house in the woods, the world will make a beaten path to his door. EMERSON

If you aren't happy with what you possess, how can you expect to be happy with what you haven't got? *Chinese Proverb*

If you have knowledge, let others light their candle by it. CICERO

If you would be wealthy, think of saving as well as getting. FRANKLIN

If you would have your business done, go; if not, send. FRANKLIN

In life, as in a football game, the principle to follow is: Hit the line hard, don't foul and don't shirk, but hit the line hard. ROOSEVELT

In the scale of destinies, brawn will never
weigh so much as brain. — LOWELL

In your minds think the truth;
In your hearts love the truth;
In your lives live the truth. — *Anonymous*

It is difficult to make a man miserable while he feels he is worthy of himself. — LINCOLN

It is easy in the world to live after the world's opinion; it is easy in solitude to live after our own; but the great man is he who in the midst of the crowd keeps with perfect sweetness the independence of solitude. — EMERSON

It is happier to be sometimes cheated than not to trust. — JOHNSON

It is impossible to be just if one is not generous. — ROUX

It is not discourteous to refuse to do wrong. — *Anonymous*

It is not enough merely to possess virtue, as if it were an art; it should be practiced. — CICERO

It is only the ignorant who despise education. — SYRUS

It may make a difference to all eternity whether we do right or wrong today. — CLARKE

Judge not thy friend until thou standest in his place. — HILLEL

Justice without wisdom is impossible. — FROUDE

Keep thy tongue from evil,
And thy lips from speaking guile.
Depart from evil, and do good;
Seek peace, and pursue it. — *Holy Bible*

A kind heart is a fountain of gladness, making everything in its vicinity freshen into smiles. — IRVING

Kindness is nobler than revenge. — SHAKESPEARE

Knowledge comes, but wisdom lingers. TENNYSON

Knowledge is power. HOBBES

Labor to keep alive in your breast that little spark of celestial fire, called Conscience. WASHINGTON

Laziness travels so slowly that poverty soon overtakes him. FRANKLIN

Let me not pray to be sheltered from dangers but to be fearless in facing them. TAGORE

Let not your mind run on what you lack as much as on what you have already. Of the things you have, select the best; and then think how eagerly they would have been sought if you did not have them. MARCUS AURELIUS

Let us have faith that right makes might; and in that faith, let us, to the end, dare to do our duty as we understand it. LINCOLN

Like a postage stamp, a man's value depends on his ability to stick to a thing till he gets there. CHAMBERLAIN

A little word in kindness spoken,
A motion or a tear,
Has often healed the heart that's broken,
And made a friend sincere. COLESWORTHY

Lives of great men all remind us
We can make our lives sublime,
And departing, leave behind us
Footprints on the sands of time. LONGFELLOW

Love all, trust a few, do wrong to none. SHAKESPEARE

Love of country is an elemental virtue, like love of home, or like honesty or courage. ROOSEVELT

Man does not live by bread alone, but by faith, by admiration, by sympathy. EMERSON

A man should never be ashamed to own he has been in the wrong, which is but saying, in other words, that he is wiser today than he was yesterday. — POPE

The man who has never been in danger cannot answer for his courage. — LA ROCHEFOUCAULD

A man's reach should exceed his grasp.
Or what's a heaven for? — BROWNING

Men of the noblest dispositions think themselves happiest when others share their happiness with them. — TAYLOR

The men who try to do something and fail are infinitely better than those who try to do nothing and succeed. — JONES

Men willingly believe what they wish. — CAESAR

A merry heart goes all the day,
A sad tires in a mile. — SHAKESPEARE

The more a man knows, the more he forgives. — *Anonymous*

Never cut what you can untie. — JOUBERT

No one can make you feel inferior without your consent. — ROOSEVELT

Nothing gives one person so much advantage over another as to remain always cool and unruffled under all circumstances. — JEFFERSON

Nothing great was ever achieved without enthusiasm. — EMERSON

Nothing is so contagious as enthusiasm; it moves stones, it charms brutes. Enthusiasm is the genius of sincerity and truth accomplishes no victories without it. — BULWER-LYTTON

O wad some power the giftie gie us
To see oursel's as ithers see us! — BURNS

Of what good to me are the things I possess and enjoy if I cannot share my enjoyment with others. *Chinese Proverb*

One loses all the time which he can employ better. ROUSSEAU

The only true source of politeness is consideration for others. SIMMS

Opinions that are opposed to mine do not offend or estrange me; they only arouse and exercise my mind. MONTAIGNE

The opportunity of a lifetime is seldom so labeled. *Anonymous*

Our country is the world — our countrymen are all mankind. GARRISON

Our greatest glory is not in never falling, but in rising every time we fall. CONFUCIUS

Patience and fortitude conquer all things. EMERSON

Patience is the art of hoping. VAUVENARGUES

Patience is the key of content. MOHAMMED

Politeness is to goodness what words are to thoughts. JOUBERT

Pride goeth before destruction, and a haughty spirit before a fall. *Holy Bible*

The problem of education is twofold; first to know and then to utter. Everyone who lives any semblance of an inner life thinks more nobly and profoundly than he speaks. STEVENSON

Reading a poor book is an opportunity lost for reading a good one. *Anonymous*

Reading makes a full man — meditation a profound man — discourse a clear man. FRANKLIN

Real difficulties can be overcome; it is only the imaginary ones that are unconquerable. VAIL

Responsiblility educates. PHILLIPS

Seek not greatness, but seek truth and you
will find both. MANN

Sense shines with a double lustre when it is
set in humility. PENN

Skillful pilots gain their reputation from storms
and tempests. EPICURUS

Small service is true service while it lasts. WORDSWORTH

So nigh is grandeur to our dust
So near is Go to man;
When Duty whispers low, "Thou must,"
The youth replies, "I can." EMERSON

Society is built unon trust. SOUTH

Solitude is as needful to the imigination as
society is wholesome for the character. LOWELL

Some people read to get away from life; others
read to get into life, to experience it more
abundantly. *Anonymous*

Speak gently; it is better far
to rule by love than fear.
Speak gently; let no harsh word mar
the good we may do here. BATES

Sullen people are the greatest possible
nuisances to themselves and to their best
friends. ARISTOTLE

Take care of the minutes for the hours will
take care of themselves . CHESTERFIELD

Tell me what company thou keepest, and I'll
tell thee what thou art. CERVANTES

There are no fragments so precious as those of
time, and none so heedlessly lost by people who
cannot make a moment, and yet can waste years. MONTGOMERY

There is as much greatness of mind in acknowledging a good turn, as in doing it. SENECA

There is more heroism in self-denial than in deeds of arms. SENECA

There is no benefit so small that a good man will not magnify it. SENECA

There is no witness so dreadful, no accuser so terrible as the conscience that dwells in the heart of every man. POLYBIUS

There is so much good in the worst of us,
And so much bad in the best of us,
That it ill behooves any of us
To find fault with the rest of us. *Anonymous*

There never was any heart truly great and gracious, that was not also tender and compassionate. SOUTH

. . . they shall beat their swords into plowshares, and their spears into pruninghooks: nation shall not lift up sword against nation, neither shall they learn war any more. *Holy Bible*

Things cannot always go your way. Learn to accept in silence the minor aggravations. OSLER

Though we travel the world over to find the beautiful we must carry it with us or we find it not. EMERSON

The three things most difficult are — to keep a secret, to forget an injury, and to make good use of leisure. CHILO

'Tis education forms the common mind;
Just as the twig is bent the tree's inclined. POPE

To give awkwardly is churlishness. The most difficult part is to give, then why not add a smile. LA BRUYERE

To look up and not down,
To look forward and not back,
To look out and not in, and
To lend a hand. — HALE

To see what is right and not to do it is want of courage. — CONFUCIUS

Tomorrow is the ambushed walk avoided by the circumspect. Tomorrow is the fatal rock on which a million ships are wrecked. — MASON

Treat your friend as if he will one day be your enemy, and your enemy as if he will one day be your friend. — LABERIUS

True humility is not a self-despising spirit; it is but a right estimate of ourselves as God sees us. — EDWARDS

The true university of these days is a collection of books. — CARLYLE

The true worth of a man is to be measured by the objects he pursues. — MARCUS AURELIUS

Under all speech that is good for anything there lies a silence that is better. Silence is deep as Eternity; speech is shallow as Time. — CARLYLE

We live by reposing trust in each other. — PLINY

We live in deeds, not years; in thoughts, not breaths; in feelings, not in figures on a dial. We should count time by heart throbs. He lives most who thinks most, feels the noblest, acts the best. — BAILEY

We must not only affirm the brotherhood of man; we must live it. — POTTER

We never know how high we are
Til we are called to rise;
And then, if we are true to plan,
Our statures touch the skies. — DICKINSON

We praise the man who is angry on the right grounds, against the right persons, in the right manner, at the right moment, and for the right length of time. — ARISTOTLE

We should render a service to a friend to bind him closer to us, and to an enemy to make a friend of him. — CLEOBULUS

A weed is a plant whose virtues have not been discovered. — EMERSON

What is beautiful is good, and who is good will soon be beautiful. — SAPPHO

When I am attacked by gloomy thoughts, nothing helps me so much as running to my books. They quickly absorb me and banish the clouds from my mind. — MONTAIGNE

When wealth is lost, nothing is lost;
When health is lost, something is lost;
When character is lost, all is lost! — *Anonymous*

When you have set yourself a task, finish it. — OVID

Where law ends, tyranny begins. — PITT

The wise man does not store up treasure. The more he gives to others the more he has for his own. — LAO-TSE

A wise man reflects before he speaks; a fool speaks, and then reflects on what he has uttered. — DELILE

The world is a looking glass and gives back to every man the reflection of his own face. Frown at it, and it in turn will look sourly upon you; laugh at it, and with it, and it is a jolly, kind companion. — THACKERAY

Write it on your heart that every day is the best day of the year. — EMERSON

You can't learn everything from experience and sometimes it's much less painful to learn from a book. SCHUMACH

You have not fulfilled every duty unless you have fulfilled that of being cheerful and pleasant. BUXTON

Your manners are always under examination, and by committees little suspected, — a police in citizens' clothes, — but are awarding or denying you very high prizes when you least think of it. EMERSON

THOUGHTS FOR THE DAY

Requiring Insight

Arranged alphabetically by first word except for A, An *and* The.

Above all, let us never forget that an act of goodness is in itself an act of happiness. It is the flower of a long inner life of joy and contentment; it tells of peaceful hours and days on the sunniest heights of our soul. MAETERLINCK

The acquisition of science is a pleasing employment. The possession of it . . . will . . . render you dear to your friends and give you fame and promotion in your own country. JEFFERSON

Admire as much as you can, most people do not admire enough. VAN GOGH

All the arts are brothers; each one is a light to the others. VOLTAIRE

America lives in the heart of every man everywhere who wishes to find a region where he will be free to work out his destiny as he chooses. WILSON

Among free men there can be no successful appeal from the ballot to the bullet, and . . . they who take such appeal are sure to lose their case and pay the cost. LINCOLN

Any fact facing us is not as important as our attitude toward it, for that determines our success or failure. The way you think about a fact may defeat you before you ever do anything about it. You are overcome by the fact because you think you are. PEALE

As I would not be a slave, so I would not be a master. This expresses my idea of democracy. Whatever differs from this, to the extent of the difference, is no democracy. LINCOLN

Be just, and fear not; let all the ends thou aimest at be thy country's, thy God's and Truth's. SHAKESPEARE

Beauty does not lie in the face. It lies in the harmony between man and his industry. Beauty is expression. When I paint a mother I try to render her beautiful by the mere look she gives her child. MILLET

Beauty is its own reward,
Being a form of Peace. NICHOLS

"Beauty is truth, truth beauty,"—that is all
Ye know on earth, and all ye need to know. KEATS

Beauty of style and harmony and grace and good rhythm depend on simplicity. PLATO

Benevolence or Justice? I do not care how benevolent the master is going to be, I will not live under a master. WILSON

The best and most important part of every man's education is that which he gives himself. GIBBON

Blessed are they who read books simply because they like to. They have the amateur spirit and they get one of the few pure pleasures an impure world affords. DE VOTO

Books are the compasses and telescopes and sextants and charts which other men have prepared to help us navigate the dangerous seas of human life. BENNETT

Books give not wisdom where was none before,
But where some is, there reading makes it more. HARINGTON

Books, those miraculous memories of high thoughts and golden moods; those magical shells, tremulous with the secrets of the ocean of life . . . those honey-combs of dreams; those orchards of knowledge; those still-beating hearts of the noble dead . . . prisms of beauty; urns stored with all the sweet of all the summers of time; immortal nightingales that sing forever to the rose of life. LE GALLIENNE

The brave man is not he who feels no fear,
For that were stupid and irrational;
But he, whose noble soul its fear subdues,
And bravely dares the danger nature shrinks from. BAILLIE

Cast thy bread upon the waters:
For thou shalt find it after many days. *Holy Bible*

A climate of freedom is most conducive to the growth of a healthy society. BARTRAM

Courage is the best gift of all; courage stands before everything. It is what preserves our liberty; safety, life, and our homes and parents, our country and children. Courage comprises all things: a man with courage has every blessing. PLAUTUS

Democracy means not "I am as good as you are," but "You are as good as I am." PARKER

Determine never to be idle. No person will have occassion to complain of the want of time who never loses any. It is wonderful how much may be done if we are always doing. JEFFERSON

Discussion is an exchange of knowledge; argument an exchange of ignorance. QUILLEN

Do not keep the alabaster boxes of your love and tenderness sealed up until your friends are dead. Fill their lives with sweetness. Speak approving, cheering words while their ears can hear them, and while their hearts can be thrilled and made happier by them. CHILDS

Do not say, when I have leisure, I shall study; thou mayest never have the leisure. HILLEL

The dogmas of the quiet past are inadequate to the stormy present. The occasion is piled high with difficulty, and we must rise with the occasion. As our case is new, so we must think anew and act anew. LINCOLN

Don't say things. What you are stands over you the while, and thunders so that I cannot hear what you say to the contrary. EMERSON

Driven from every other corner of the earth, freedom of thought and the right of private judgment in matters of conscience direct their course to this happy country as their last asylum. ADAMS

Education alone can conduct us to that enjoyment which is at once best in quality and infinite in quantity. MANN

Education is the leading human souls to what is best, and making what is best about of them; and these two objects are always attainable together, and by the same means. The training which makes men happiest in themselves also makes them most serviceable to others. RUSKIN

Employ thy time well, if thou meanest to gain leisure. FRANKLIN

Every good citizen makes his country's honor his own, and cherishes it not only as precious, but as sacred. JACKSON

Experience shows that success is due less to ability than to zeal. BUXTON

The fame of great men ought always to be estimated by the means used to acquire it. LA ROCHEFOUCAULD

Fellow citizens, we cannot escape history. We will be remembered in spite of ourselves. No personal significance or insignificance can spare one or another of us. The fiery trial through which we pass will light us down, in honor or dishonor, to the latest generation. LINCOLN

A fool must be known by six things: anger, without cause; speech, without profit; change, without progress; inquiry, without object; putting trust in a stranger, and mistaking foes for friends. *Arabian Proverb*

For books are more than books, they are the life, the very heart and core of ages past, the reason why men lived and worked and died, the essence and quintessence of their lives. LOWELL

For I have sworn upon the altar of God, eternal hostility against every form of tyranny over the mind of man. JEFFERSON

Freedom today is something more than being let alone. The program of a government of freedom must in these days be positive, not negative merely. WILSON

God grants liberty only to those who love it, and are always ready to guard and defend it. WEBSTER

A good example is the best sermon. FULLER

Good order is the foundation of all good things. BURKE

Great men are they who see that spiritual is stronger than any material force, that thoughts rule the world. EMERSON

Great minds, like heaven, are pleased in doing good. ROWE

The greatest of faults, I should say, is to be conscious of none. CARLYLE

Happiness is a form of courage. JACKSON

Happy is he who looks only into his work to know if it will succeed, never into the times or the public opinion; and who writes from the love of imparting certain thoughts and not from the necessity of sale—who writes always to the unknown friend. EMERSON

Happy the man, and happy he alone,
He who can call today his own;
He who, secure within, can say,
Tomorrow, do thy worst, for I have lived today. DRYDEN

He that cannot forgive others, breaks the bridge over which he must pass himself; for every man has need to be forgiven. HERBERT

He who is plenteously provided for from within needs little from without. GOETHE

He who receives an idea from me receives instruction himself without lessening mine; as he who lights his taper at mine receives light without darkening me. JEFFERSON

He who reigns within himself, and rules passions, desires and fear, is more than a king. MILTON

He who waits to do a great deal of good at once, will never do anything. JOHNSON

Heaven is not reached at a single bound;
But we build the ladder by which we rise
From the lowly earth to the vaulted skies,
And we mount to its summit round by round. HOLLAND

Honest men fear neither the light nor the dark. *Anonymous*

I agree with you that there is a natural aristocracy among men. The grounds of this are virtue and talents. JEFFERSON

I am more and more convinced that our happiness lies in the way we meet the events of life and not in the events themselves. HUMBOLDT

I disapprove of what you say, but I will defend to the death your right to say it. VOLTAIRE

I expect to pass through this world but once. Any good therefore that I can do, or any kindness that I can show to any fellow creature, let me do it now. Let me not defer or neglect it, for I shall not pass this way again. GRELLET

I have always believed that good is only beauty put into practice. ROUSSEAU

I have never been able to conceive how any rational being could propose happiness to himself from the exercise of power over others. JEFFERSON

I hope I shall always posses firmness and virtue enough to maintain what I consider the most enviable of all titles, the character of an "honest man." WASHINGTON

I know no safe depository of the ultimate powers of society but the people themselves; and if we think them not enlightened enough to exercise their control with a wholesome discretion, the remedy is not to take it from them, but to inform their discretion by education. JEFFERSON

I love my country's good, with a respect more tender, more holy and profound than my own life. SHAKESPEARE

I was eyes to the blind,
And feet was I to the lame.
I was a father to the poor:
And the cause which I knew
not I searched out. *Holy Bible*

I will govern my life and my thoughts, as if the whole world were to see the one, and to read the other. SENECA

Ideals are like stars; you will not succeed in touching them with your hands. But like the seafaring man on the desert of waters, you choose them as your guides, and following them you will reach your destiny. SCHURZ

If a man does not keep pace with his companions, perhaps it is because he hears a different drummer. Let him step to the music which he hears, however measured or far away. THOREAU

If a man is sincere he will seek earnestly for the truth. KEMPIS

If all our wishes were gratified, most of our pleasures would be destroyed. WHATELY

If humility and purity be not in the heart, they are not in the home: and if they are not in the home, they are not in the City. ELIOT

If the day and the night are such that you greet them with joy and life emits a fragrance like flowers and sweet scented herbs, is more elastic, more starry, more immortal — that is your success. THOREAU

If we have not peace within ourselves, it is in vain to seek it from outward sources. LA ROCHEFOUCAULD

If you once forfeit the confidence of your fellow citizens, you can never regain their respect and esteem. It is true that you may fool all the people some of the time; you can even fool some of the people all the time; but you can't fool all of the people all the time. LINCOLN

If you wish success in life, make perseverance your bosom friend, experience your wise counsellor, caution your elder brother, and hope your guardian genius. ADDISON

Ignorance is the night of the mind, but a night without moon or star. CONFUCIUS

In great attempts it is glorious even to fail. LONGINUS

Inspiration comes of working every day. BAUDELAIRE

It is chiefly through books that we enjoy intercourse with superior minds... In the best books, great men talk to us, give us their most precious thoughts, and pour their souls into ours. CHANNING

It is impossible to understand oneself without understanding others, and impossible to understand others without understanding oneself. HARRIS

It is only through the morning gate of the beautiful that you can penetrate into the realm of knowledge. That which we feel here as beauty we shall one day know as truth. SCHILLER

It matters not how a man dies, but how he lives. JOHNSON

Knowledge is the treasure, but judgment the treasurer, of a wise man. PENN

Learning makes a man fit company for himself. YOUNG

The legitimate object of government is to do for a community of people whatever they need to have done but cannot do at all, or cannot so well do for themselves in their separate and individual capacities. LINCOLN

Leisure without study is death; it is a tomb for the living. SENECA

Liberty, after she has been chained up awhile, is always more fierce, and sets her teeth in deeper than she could otherwise have done if she had never been restrained. CICERO

Life is made up, not of great sacrifices or duties but of little things, in which smiles and kindnesses and small obligations, given habitually, are what win and preserve the heart and secure comfort.

DAVY

A little learning is a dangerous thing.

POPE

A man is never so on trial as in the moment of good fortune.

WALLACE

A man is rich in proportion to the number of things which he can afford to let alone.

THOREAU

Many people think they will become good by doing no harm; that's a lie.

VAN GOGH

Many things are not attempted because they appear difficult and dangerous; many things appear difficult and dangerous only because they are not attempted.

KAUNITZ

Men, like bullets, go furthest when polished.

RICHTER

The more we do, the more we can do; the more busy we are, the more leisure we have.

HAZLITT

The most evident sign of wisdom is continued cheerfulness.

MONTAIGNE

A nation is great not through dams in its rivers, or its ships on the seas, or the deposits in its banks. It is great by the moral fiber and character of its citizens. Nations die when these weaken.

HOOVER

A nation which cherishes the freedom of its citizens will try to give all its children an education. It will try to give them the kind of education that leads to understanding.

HUTCHINS

Never bear more than one kind of trouble at a time. Some people bear three — all they have had, all they have now,, and all they expect to have.

HALE

No life can be pure in its purpose and strong in its strife and all life not be purer and stronger thereby.

MEREDITH

No matter what his rank or position may be, the lover of books is the richest and happiest of the children of men. LANGFORD

Nobody can cheat us as we cheat ourselves;
Nobody can deceive us as we deceive ourselves;
Nobody can defeat us as we defeat ourselves. HARRIS

Oh, the comfort, the inexpressible comfort of feeling safe with a person, having neither to weigh thoughts nor measure words, but pouring them all right out, just as they are, chaff and grain together; certain that a faithful hand will take and sift them, keeep what is worth keeping, and then with the breath of kindness blow the rest away. CRAIK

One cannot always be a hero, but one can always be a man. GOETHE

One of the illusions of life is that the present hour is not the critical, decisive hour. Write it on your heart that every day is the best day. EMERSON

One of the sublimest things in the world is plain truth. BULWER-LYTTON

Only what we have wrought into our character during life can we take away with us. HUMBOLDT

Opportunity is ever worth expecting; let your hook be ever hanging ready. The fish will be in the pool where you least imagine it to be. OVID

The ornaments of a house are the friends that frequent it. GOETHE

Our country, right or wrong. When right, to be kept right; when wrong, to be put right. SCHURZ

Our country — this great republic means nothing unless it means the triumph of a real democracy, the triumph of popular government, and in the long run, of and economic system under which each man shall be guaranteed the opportunity to show the best that there is in him. ROOSEVELT

Our native land charms us with inexpressible sweetness, and never allows us to forget that we belong to it. — OVID

Our reliance is in the love if liberty which God has planted in us. Our defense is in the spirit which prizes liberty as the heritage of all men, in all lands everywhere. — LINCOLN

Pass not judgment upon thy neighbor until thou are come into his place. — HILLEL

Patience does not mean indifference. We may work and trust and wait, but we ought not to be idle or careless while waiting. — HAMILTON

Peace and order and security and liberty are safe so long as love of country burns in the hearts of the people. — MCKINLEY

Peace is the natural state of man. — THOMSON

The pedigree of honey
Does not concern the bee;
A clover, anytime, to him
Is aristocracy. — DICKINSON

The pen is mightier than the sword. — BULWER-LYTTON

People are not usually better than the books they read. — *Anonymous*

Philosophy becomes poetry, and science imagination, in the enthusiasm of genius. — DISRAELI

Politeness and good-breeding are absolutely necessary to adorn any, or all other good qualities or talents... The scholar, without good-breeding, is a pedant; the philosopher, a cynic; the soldier, a brute; and every man disagreeable. — CHESTERFIELD

The power of a man increases steadily by continuance in one direction. — EMERSON

Prefer diligence before idleness, unless you esteem rust before brightness. — PLATO

Procrastination is the thief of time. — YOUNG

Qualities of the heart, not those of the face, should attract us. — LAMARTINE

The real object of education is to give children resources that will endure as long as life endures; habits that time will ameliorate, not destroy; occupation that will render sickness tolerable, solitude pleasant, age venerable, life more dignified and useful, and death less terrible. — SMITH

Right in the course of marching feet is an idea whose hour has come. — HUGO

Self-control is the greatest of victories. — PLATO

The silence that accepts merit as the most natural thing in the world, is the highest applause. — EMERSON

The similarities between people are much greater than the differences; differences are accidental, similarities are essential. — HARRIS

So my first tip on reading is simply this: Be a reader. Read anything and everything, the more the better. Keep a book on the fire of your mind all the time. Follow your fancy. Read books you like. Then, for a change, read a book you don't like — you may stumble into a new world. — FLESCH

Some books are to be tasted, others to be swallowed, and some few to be chewed and digested. — BACON

Such as are thy habitual thoughts, such also will be the character of thy mind; for the soul is dyed by the thoughts. Think then these thoughts: goodness, mercy, charity. — MARCUS AURELIUS

Tell me what you read, and I'll tell you what you are. — *Anonymous*

There are many qualities which we need alike in private citizen and in public man, but three above all, three for the lack of which no brilliancy and no genius can atone — and those three are courage, honesty, and common sense. — ROOSEVELT

There is a certain relief in change, even though it be from bad to worse; as I have found in travelling in a stagecoach, that it is often a comfort to shift one's position and be bruised in a new place. IRVING

There is a destiny that makes us brothers
None goes his way alone;
All that we send into the lives of others
Comes back into our own. MARKHAM

There is a tide in the affairs of men,
Which, taken at the flood, leads on to fortune;
Omitted, all the voyage of their life
Is bound in shallows and in miseries. SHAKESPEARE

There is a time in every man's education when he arrives at the conviction that envy is ignorance; that imitation is suicide; that he must take himself, for better of for worse, as his portion; that, though the wide universe is full of good, no kernel or nourishing corn can come to him but through his toil bestowed on that plot of ground which is given him to till. EMERSON

A thoughtful mind, when it sees the nation's flag, sees not the flag only, but the nation itself. BEECHER

Time is money. FRANKLIN

'Tis more brave
To live, than to die. BULWER-LYTTON

To err is human, to forgive divine. POPE

To make knowledge valuable, you must have the cheerfulness of wisdom. EMERSON

To my mind, the best and most faultless character is his who is as ready to pardon the rest of mankind, as though he daily transgressed himself; and at the same time as cautious to avoid a fault as if he never forgave one. PLINY THE YOUNGER

To the fool, he who speaks wisdom will sound foolish. EURIPIDES

True politeness consists in being easy one's self, and in making every one about one as easy as one can. POPE

The true test of a civilization is, not the census, nor the size of cities, nor the crops — no, but the kind of man the country turns out. EMERSON

Trust men, and they will be true to you; treat them greatly, and they will show themselves great. EMERSON

We are all ignorant. We are just ignorant about different things. ROGERS

We are only certain of today — yesterday is gone and tomorrow is always coming. VANBEE

We see only what we know. GOETHE

We will be happy if we can get around to the idea that art is not an outside and extra thing; that it is a natural outcome of a state of being; that the state of being is the important thing; that a man can be a carpenter and be a great man. HENRI

What a man thinks of himself, that it is which determines, or rather indicates his fate. THOREAU

When all else is lost, the future still remains. BOVEE

When any duty is to be done, it is fortunate for you if you feel like doing it; but, if you do not feel like it, that is no reason for not doing it. GLADDEN

When love and skill work together expect a masterpiece. RUSKIN

When we are unhurried and wise, we perceive that only great and worthy things have any permanent and absolute existence, that petty fears and petty pleasures are but the shadow of reality. THOREAU

While we are postponing, life speeds by. SENECA

The wisest man could ask no more of Fate
Than to be simple, modest, manly, true,
Safe from the Many, honored by the Few;
To count as naught in World, or Church, or State,
But inwardly in secret to be great. LOWELL

Words are the dress of thoughts; which should no more be presented in rags, tatters and dirt, than your person should. CHESTERFIELD

Worthy books
Are not companions — they are solitudes:
We lose ourselves in them and all our cares. BAILEY

A CALENDAR
OF SPECIAL DAYS AND WEEKS

SPECIAL DAYS AND WEEKS

This list is presented merely as a selection for the convenience of teachers and principals—or committees. Unless otherwise indicated the dates listed are birth dates. For other interesting or important events see the articles under the names of the months of the year in *The World Book Encyclopedia* and the article "Festivals and Holidays" in *Compton's Pictured Encyclopedia*. See also the index of *The World Almanac* under "Holidays."

SEPTEMBER

	Labor Day (1st Monday)
2	V-J Day
6	Marquis de La Fayette
9	Admission Day, California
11	O. Henry
12	Defenders Day, Maryland
13	John Barry Day (Pennsylvania)
14	National Anthem Day
15	James Fenimore Cooper
16	Alfred Noyes
17	Citizenship Day
21	First Day of Autumn
22	Emancipation Day
	American Indian Day (4th Friday)
28	Frances E. Willard

OCTOBER

7	James Whitcomb Riley
10	Guiseppe Verdi
11	General Pulaski Day
12	Columbus Day
14	Dwight D. Eisenhower
15	Poetry Day
17	Battle of Saratoga (1777)
21	Samuel Taylor Coleridge
24	William Penn Day
24	United Nations Day
27	Theodore Roosevelt
28	Liberty Day (Statue of Liberty dedicated)
28	Dr. Jonas Salk
30	John Adams
31	John Keats

October

31 Nevada Day, Nevada
31 Halloween

United Nations Week

November

3 William Cullen Bryant
7 Marie Curie
11 Veterans Day
13 Robert Louis Stevenson
19 Lincoln's Gettysburg Address (1863)
25 Andrew Carnegie
29 Louisa May Alcott
30 Jonathan Swift
30 Winston S. Churchill
30 Samuel Clemens

Thanksgiving Day (4th Thursday)
Election Day (1st Tuesday after 1st Monday)

American Art Week
American Education Week
Book Week

December

2 First Nuclear Chain Reaction (1942)
5 Bill of Rights (First 10 amendments to the Constitution went into effect, 1791)
7 Japanese Bomb Pearl Harbor (1941)
8 Jan Sibelius
10 Human Rights Day
12 William Lloyd Garrison
16 Ludwig van Beethoven
17 Wright Brothers Day
17 John Greenleaf Whittier
21 First Day of Winter
21 Pilgrims landed at Plymouth (1620)
22 Forefathers' Day
24 Christopher "Kit" Carson
25 Clara Barton
28 Woodrow Wilson
30 Rudyard Kipling

Bill of Rights Week

January

1 New Year's Day
1 Betsy Ross
6 Twelfth Night
6 Carl Sandburg
11 Alexander Hamilton
12 John Hancock
13 Stephen C. Foster (Died, 1864)
14 Albert Schweitzer
17 Benjamin Franklin
18 Daniel Webster
19 Edgar Allan Poe
19 Robert E. Lee
20 Inauguration Day (every 4th year)
22 Lord Byron
25 Robert Burns
27 Wolfgang Amadeus Mozart
27 Lewis Caroll
30 Franklin D. Roosevelt
31 Franz Schubert

Child Labor Day (last Sunday)

George Washington Carver Week

March of Dimes Month

February

1 National Freedom Day
3 Four Chaplains Memorial Day
4 Charles A. Lindbergh
5 Felix Mendelssohn-Bartholdy
6 Aaron Burr
7 Charles Dickens
8 Boy Scout Day
10 Charles Lamb
11 Thomas Alva Edison
12 Abraham Lincoln
14 Frederick Douglass
14 St. Valentine's Day
15 Susan B. Anthony
15 U.S.S. Maine sunk in Havana harbor (1898)

FEBRUARY

19 Nicolaus Copernicus
22 George Washington
22 Frederic Chopin
22 James Russell Lowell
22 Edna St. Vincent Millay
26 Victor Hugo
27 Henry Wadsworth Longfellow

Boy Scout Week
Brotherhood Week
Negro History Week

MARCH

2 Texas Independence Day
3 William Penn received grant of Pennsylvania (1681)
6 Alamo Day
6 Buonarroti Michelangelo
6 Elizabeth Barrett Browning
7 Luther Burbank
14 Albert Einstein
15 Charter Day (Pennsylvania)
15 Andrew Jackson
16 James Madison
17 Evacuation Day (1776)
17 St. Patrick's Day
18 John C. Calhoun
21 First Day of Spring
21 Johann Sebastian Bach
23 Patrick Henry declared, "Give me liberty, or give me death!"
26 Robert Frost
26 Kuhio Day, Hawaii
30 Seward Day, Alaska
31 Franz Joseph Haydn

Girl Scout Week
National Wildlife Week

APRIL

2 Hans Christian Andersen
3 Washington Irving
5 Booker T. Washington
6 Raphael

April

6 America Enters World War I (1917)
7 William Wordsworth
9 Appomattox Day
12 Henry Clay
13 Thomas Jefferson
14 Pan-American Day
15 Leonardo da Vinci
18 Paul Revere's Ride
19 Patriot's Day (Battle of Lexington and Concord)
22 Oklahoma Day
23 Edwin Markham
23 William Shakespeare
25 Walter de la Mare
25 Guglielmo Marconi
27 Samuel F. B. Morse
27 U. S. Grant
28 James Monroe

Arbor Day
Bird Day

National Library Week

May

1 May Day
4 Horace Mann
7 Johannes Brahms
7 Peter Ilyich Tschaikovsky
7 Robert Browning
8 V-E Day
8 Harry S. Truman
12 Florence Nightingale
14 Settlement of Jamestown
20 Honore de Balzac
22 Richard Wagner
25 Ralph Waldo Emerson
27 Julia Ward Howe
28 William Pitt
29 Patrick Henry
29 John F. Kennedy
30 Memorial Day
31 Walt Whitman

May

Armed Forces Day (3rd Saturday)
Mother's Day (2nd Sunday)

Be kind to Animals Week (1st week)
Poppy Week
Music Week

June

3 Jefferson Davis
6 D-Day
6 Nathan Hale
11 Kamehameka Day, Hawaii
14 Flag Day
14 Harriet Beecher Stowe
15 Edvard Grieg
17 Bunker Hill Day
18 Battle of Waterloo
19 King John signed the Magna Carta
20 West Virginia Day
21 First Day of Summer
23 Penn's Treaty with the Indians

Father's Day (3rd Sunday)

Major Religious Holidays and Holy Days

All Saints' Day, November 1
Christmas, December 25
Epiphany, January 6
Good Friday
Easter

Eastern Orthodox Christmas, January 7
Eastern Orthodox Easter

Purim (drawing of lots), usually in March
Passover, March or April
Pentecost, fifth day after Passover
Rosh Hashana (New Year), September or October
Yom Kippur (Day of Atonement), September or October

Channukah or Hanukkah or Feast of Dedication
(Feast of Lights), December

APPENDIX I

I PLEDGE ALLEGIANCE

*Suggestions for Introducing the Pledge of Allegiance**

Today, let us salute the flag in honor of our founding fathers who had visions of today's America.

Join me in saluting the flag of our country, the emblem of truth and justice!

When we realize what our flag stands for, it is with genuine enthusiasm we salute the flag our country.

We will now salute the emblem of America, the flag of the United States.

Because we are thankful and appreciative of America's role in world leadership, let us now salute our flag!

For the opportunities our country offers to the youth of America, let us now salute our flag, the emblem of our nation.

For those who died that this nation might live, let us now salute our flag.

We, the people — that's what our flag stands for: Let us salute our flag!

To secure the blessings of liberty to ourselves and our posterity is a challenge to all of us. Let us salute our flag!

In the folds of our flag are enshrined every ideal, hope, and opportunity made possible because someone has lived. Let us salute our flag!

Our state is represented by one of the fifty stars on our flag. Let us now pledge allegiance to our flag as individuals and together for our state.

The flag of the United States of America is the emblem of our nation — the leader of the free world. Let us now salute our flag!

---

* *Used with permission of the author, Paul S. Chance, Vice Principal, Los Angeles City Schools.*

In peace and war our flag lies proudly because Americans are not forgetful of others. Join me in saluting our flag.

We have good government only when we, the people of the United States, play an active part in making it good. Let us salute our flag, the emblem of our country.

The greatest public document of the American people is the Constitution of the United States. Our flag represents our Constitution in action. Let us now salute the flag.

Where our flag flies, there is less oppression and more opportunity for self-expression. Will you now join me in expressing your allegiance to the flag?

APPENDIX II

SOME MUSIC FOR OPENING EXERCISES

Songs to Start a Day

Best Things in Life Are Free
Climb Every Mountain
Getting to Know You
Hills of Home
House I Live In
I Whistle a Happy Tune
Look for the Silver Lining
My Favorite Things
No Man Is an Island
Oh, What a Beautiful Mornin'
Over the Rainbow
Sound of Music
You'll Never Walk Alone
Work for the Night Is Coming

Songs for Holidays Through the School Year

Colombus Day

NEW MUSIC HORIZONS — Fourth Book

Three Little Ships 21

Thanksgiving

In many music books
Come, Ye Thankful People Come

Hanukkah

UNION SONGSTER

In the Candles' Rays 258
Oh Hanukkah, Oh Hanukkah 262
Rock of Ages 257
Who Can Retell? 260

Christmas

PAGE

Purim

Easter

Passover

Patriotic Songs

In many music books or sheet music

America
America the Beautiful
Columbia, the Gem of the Ocean
The Star-Spangled Banner
You're a Grand Old Flag

Recordings

BACH, J. S., *Concertos Numbers 1, 2, 3, 4 for Harpsichord*

BARBER, SAMUEL, Adagio for Strings

BEETHOVEN, LUDWIG VAN, *Symphony Number 6* (1st movement)

BRAHMS, JOHANNES, *Alto Rhapsody, Opus 53*

Variations on a Theme by Handel, Opus 24

CORELLI, ARCANGELO, *Concerti grossi, Opus 5*

COUPERIN, FRANÇOIS, *Lamentations of Jeremiah*

DEBUSSY, CLAUDE, *Clair de lune*

DELIUS, FREDERIC, *Walk to Paradise Garden*

GRIEG, EDVARD, *Peer Gynt Suites Number 1 and Number 2*

HANDEL, GEORGE F., *Concerti grossi, Opus 6* (1-12)

HAYDN, FRANZ JOSEPH, *Surprise Symphony* (2nd movement)

MOZART, WOLFGANG, *Eine kleine Nachtmusik* (2nd movement)

PROKOFIEV, SERGE, *Overture on Hebrew Themes, Opus 67*

PURCELL, HENRY, *Sonata in D for Trumpet and Strings.*

RAVEL, MAURICE, *Pavane pour une infante défunte*

APPENDIX III

SELECTED BIBLIOGRAPHY

SELECTED BIBLIOGRAPHY OF THE MOST USEFUL BOOKS FOR OPENING EXERCISES

Kindergarten—3

ANGLUND, JOAN WALSH, *Love Is a Special Way of Feeling*. New York, Harcourt, Brace and World, Inc., 1960.

ANGLUND, JOAN WALSH, *A Friend Is Someone Who Likes You*. New York, Harcourt, Brace and World, Inc., 1958.

BARKSDALE, LENA, *The First Thanksgiving*. New York, Alfred A. Knopf, Inc., 1942.

BEHN, HARRY, *The Little Hill*. New York, Harcourt, Brace and World, Inc., 1949.

DALGLIESH, ALICE, *The Columbus Story*. New York, Charles Scribner's Sons, 1955.

DALGLIESH, ALICE, *Courage of Sarah Noble*. New York, Charles Scribner's Sons, 1954.

DOANE, PELAGIE, *A Small Child's Book of Verse*. New York, Oxford University Press, Inc., 1948.

FYLEMAN, ROSE, *Fairies and Chimneys*. New York, George H. Doran, 1920.

GEISMER, BARBARA, and ANTOINETTE SUTER, *Very Young Verses*. Boston, Houghton Mifflin Company, 1945.

GEORGIADY, NICHOLAS, and LOUIS ROMANO, *Our Country's Flag*. Chicago, Follett Publishing Company, 1963.

MCGOVERN, ANN, *Why It's a Holiday*. New York, Random House, 1960.

MILNE, A. A., *When We Were Very Young*. New York, E. P. Dutton and Company, 1924.

REES, ELINOR, *About Our Flag*. Chicago, Melmont Publishers, Inc., 1960.

ROSSETTI, CHRISTINA GEORGINA, *Sing-Song*. New York, The Macmillan Company, 1952.

SCARRY, RICHARD, *The Fables of La Fontaine*. Garden City, Doubleday and Company, Inc., 1963.

STUART, JESSE, *A Penny's Worth of Character*. New York, McGraw-Hill Book Company, Inc., 1954.

STEVENSON, ROBERT LOUIS, *A Child's Garden of Verses*. New York, Wonder Books, Inc., 1958.

Kindergarten—6

ARBUTHNOT, MAY HILL, *Time for Poetry*. Chicago, Scott, Foresman and Company, 1952.

Association for Childhood Education, *Sung Under the Silver Umbrella*. New York, The Macmillan Company, 1935.

BREWTON, SARA, and JOHN E. BREWTON, *Sing a Song of Seasons*. New York. The Macmillan Company, 1955.

BURNETT, BERNICE, *First Book of Holidays*. New York, Franklin Watts, Inc., 1955.

DALGLIESH, ALICE, *The Thanksgiving Story*. New York , Charles Scribner's Sons, 1954.

HARRINGTON, MILDRED, *Ring-a-round*. New York, The Macmillan Company, 1930.

HUFFARD, GRACE T., and others, *My Poetry Book*. New York, Holt, Rinehart and Winston, Inc., 1956.

MCFARLAND, WILMA, *For a Child*. Philadelphia, Westminster Press, 1947.

MACK, SARA, *Inspirational Readings for Elementary Grades*. Kutztown, The Kutztown Publishing Company, Inc., 1964.

MILLER, NATALIE, *The Story of the Statue of Liberty*. Chicago, Childrens Press, Inc., 1965.

O'NEIL, MARY, *Hailstones and Halibut Bones*. Garden City, Doubleday and Company, Inc., 1961.

PETERSON, ISABEL J., *The First Book of Poetry*. New York, Franklin Watts, Inc., 1954.

THOMPSON, BLANCHE J., *More Silver Pennies. New York,* The Macmillan Company, 1939.

THOMPSON, BLANCHE J., *Silver Pennies.* New York, The Macmillan Company, 1926.

THOMPSON, JEAN MCKEE, *Poems to Grow On.* Boston, Beacon Press, Inc., 1957.

UNTERMEYER, LOUIS, *Rainbow in the Sky.* New York, Harcourt, Brace and World, Inc., 1935.

WERNER, JANE, *The Golden Book of Poetry.* New York, Golden Press, Inc., 1949.

Kindergarten—9

SECHRIST, ELIZABETH H., *One Thousand Poems for Children.* Philadelphia, Macrae Smith Company, 1946.

UNTERMEYER, LOUIS, *Golden Treasury of Poetry.* New York, Golden Press, Inc., 1959.

Grades 4—6

CATHON, LAURA E., and THUSNELDA, SCHMIDT, *Treasured Tales.* Nashville, Abingdon Press, 1960.

EIBLING, H. H., and others, *Great Names in Our Country's Story.* River Forest, Laidlaw Brothers, 1959.

LAWSON, ROBERT, *Watchwords of Liberty.* Boston, Little, Brown and Company, 1943.

MCNEER, MAY, *Armed with Courage.* Nashville, Abingdon Press, 1957.

PETERSHAM, MAUD, *Story of the Presidents of the United States of America.* New York, The Macmillan Company, 1953.

THOMAS, JOSEPHINE H., *Our Holidays in Poetry.* New York, H. W. Wilson Company, 1929.

WITTY, PAUL, *You and the Constitution of the United States.* Chicago, Childrens Press, Inc., 1948.

Grades 4—9

ADAMS, FLORENCE, *Highdays and Holidays*. New York, E. P. Dutton and Company, 1927.

BENÉT, ROSEMARY, and STEPHEN VINCENT BENÉT, *A Book of Americans*. New York, Farrar, Straus and Company, 1933.

BROWN, HARRIET, and JOSEPH GUADAGNOLO, *America Is My Country*. Boston, Houghton Mifflin Company, 1955.

CHASE, ALICE E., *Famous Paintings*. New York, Platt and Munk Company, Inc., 1951.

COLE WILLIAMS, *Poems for Seasons and Celebrations*. Cleveland, World Publishing Company, 1963.

COLE, WILLIAMS, *The Birds and the Beasts Were There*. Cleveland, World Publishing Company, 1961.

COOK, ROY J., *One Hundred and One Famous Poems*. Chicago, Reilly and Lee, 1916.

DESMOND, ALICE CURTIS, *Your Flag and Mine*. New York, The Macmillan Company, 1960.

FITCH, FLORENCE MARY, *One God: The Ways We Worship Him*. New York, Lothrop, Lee and Shepard Company, Inc., 1944.

LYONS, JOHN HENRY, *Stories of Our American Patriotic Songs*. New York, Vanguard Press, Inc., 1942.

MCSPADDEN, J. WALKER, *The Book of Holidays*. New York, Thomas Y. Crowell Company, 1958.

READ, HERBERT, *This Way, Delight*. New York, Pantheon Books, 1956.

RICHARDSON, BEN, *Great American Negroes*. New York, Thomas Y. Crowell Company, 1956.

ROSS, GEORGE E., *Know Your Declaration of Independence*. Chicago, Rand McNally and Company, 1963.

ROSS, GEORGE E., *Know Your Presidents and Their Wives*. Chicago, Rand McNally and Company, 1960.

SECHRIST, ELIZABETH H., *It's Time for Brotherhood.* Philadelphia, Macrae Smith Company, 1962.

SECHRIST, ELIZABETH H., *Poems for Red Letter Days.* Philadelphia, Macrae Smith Company, 1951.

TEASDALE, SARA, *Stars Tonight.* New York, The Macmillan Company, 1930.

UNTERMEYER, LOUIS, *Stars to Steer By.* New York, Harcourt, Brace and World, Inc., 1926.

UNTERMEYER, LOUIS, *This Singing World.* New York, Harcourt, Brace and World, Inc., 1926.

WIGGIN, KATE D., and NORA A. SMITH, *Golden Number.* Garden City, Doubleday and Company, Inc., 1910.

Grades 4—12

ADSHEAD, GLADYS L., *An Inheritance of Poetry.* Boston, Houghton Mifflin Company, 1948.

BARTLETT, JOHN, *Familiar Quotations.* Boston, Little, Brown and Company, 1955.

BARTLETT, JOHN, *Shorter Bartlett's Familiar Quotations.* Boston, Little, Brown and Company, 1953.

COPELAND, LEWIS, *Popular Quotations for All Uses.* Garden City, Doubleday and Company, Inc., 1961.

DOUGLAS, G. W., *The American Book of Days.* New York, H. W. Wilson Company, 1948.

FERRIS, HELEN, *Favorite Poems Old and New.* Garden City, Doubleday and Company, Inc., 1957.

FROST, ROBERT, *Complete Poems.* New York, Holt, Rinehart and Winston, Inc., 1956.

GANNET, LEWIS, *The Family Book of Verse.* New York, Harper and Row, Publishers, Inc., 1961.

GINIGER, KENNETH, *America, America, America.* New York, Franklin Watts, Inc., 1957.

HARRINGTON, MILDRED P., and JOSEPHINE H. THOMAS, *Our Holidays in Poetry*. New York, H. W. Wilson Company, 1929.

HOKE, HELEN, *Patriotism, Patriotism, Patriotism*. New York, Franklin Watts, Inc., 1963.

STEVENSON, BURTON E., *Home Book of Quotations*. New York, Dodd, Mead and Company, 1958.

STEVENSON, BURTON E., *The Home Book of Verse for Young Folks*. New York, Holt, Rinehart and Winston, Inc., 1929.

TEASDALE, SARA, *Flame and Shadow*. New York, The Macmillan Company, 1920.

Grades 7—12

BARROWS, MARJORIE, *One Thousand Beautiful Things*. New York, Hawthorn Books, Inc., 1947.

CARHART, GEORGE S., *Through Magic Casements*. New York, The Macmillan Company, 1926.

COMMAGER, HENRY STEELE, *Documents of American History*. New York, Appleton-Century-Crofts, Inc., 1963.

FREUND, MIRIAM, *Jewels for a Crown*. New York, McGraw-Hill Book Company, 1963.

KIERAN, JOHN, *Poems to Remember*. Garden City, Doubleday and Company, Inc., 1945.

MORRIS, RICHARD B., *Basic Documents in American History*. Princeton, D. Van Nostrand Company, Inc., 1956.

MORRIS, RICHARD B., *Voices from America's Past,* Volumes I-III. New York, E. P. Dutton and Company, 1963.

National Education Asociation Citizenship Committee, *American Citizens Handbook*. Washington, D. C., National Education Association, 1951.

NICHOLS, WILLIAM, *A New Treasury of Words to Live By*. New York, Simon and Schuster, Inc., 1959.

NICHOLS WILLIAM, *Third Book of Words to Live By*. New York, Simon and Schuster, Inc., 1962.

NICHOLS, WILLIAM, *Words to Live By*. New York, Simon and Schuster, Inc., 1949.

ORCHARD, NORRIS E., *Study Successfully*. New York, MacGraw-Hill Book Company, 1953.

ROBERTS, KATE LOUISE, *Hoyt's New Encyclopedia of Practical Quotations*. New York, Funk and Wagnalls Company, 1940.

SANDBURG, CARL, *Complete Poems*. New York, Harcourt, Brace and World, Inc., 1950.

Saturday Evening Post, *Adventures of the Mind, First Series*. New York, Alfred A. Knopf, Inc., 1959.

Saturday Evening Post, *Adventures of the Mind, Second Series*. New York, Alfred A. Knopf, Inc., 1961.

VAN DOREN, CARL, *Patriotic Anthology*. Garden City, Doubleday and Company, Inc., 1941.

WARD, HERMAN M., *Poems for Pleasure*. New York, Hill and Wang, Inc., 1963.

Grades 10–12

EMERSON, RALPH WALDO, *Essays*. New York, Hawthorn Books, Inc., 1936.

FADIMAN, CLIFTON, *The American Treasury, 1455-1955*. New York, Harper and Row, Publishers, Inc., 1955.

GIBRAN, KAHLIL, *The Prophet*. New York, Alfred A. Knopf, Inc., 1929.

GIBRAN, KAHLIL, *The Voice of the Master*. New York, Citadel Press, 1958.

Hallmark Cards, *Poetry for Pleasure*. Garden City, Doubldeay and Company, Inc., 1960.

HUTCHISON, RUTH, and RUTH ADAMS, *Every Day's a Holiday*. New York, Harper and Row, Publishers, Inc., 1951.

Kazin, Alfred, and Daniel Aaron, *Emerson, A Modern Anthology*. Boston, Houghton Mifflin Company, 1958.

Markham, Edwin, *The Man with the Hoe, Lincoln, and Other Poems*. Garden City, Doubleday and Company, Inc., 1899.

Murrow, Edward, *This I Believe*. New York, Simon and Schuster, Inc., 1952.

Paulmier, Hilah, and Robert H. Schauffler, *Good Will Days*. New York, Dodd, Mead and Company, 1947.

Peterson, Wilfred, *The Art of Living*. New York, Simon and Schuster, Inc., 1961.

Peterson, Wilfred, *The New Book of the Art of Living*. New York, Simon and Schuster, Inc., 1963.

Rapport, Samuel B., *Light for the Road*. New York, Harper and Row, Publishers, Inc., 1961.

Untermeyer, Louis, *Modern American Poetry*. New York, Harcourt, Brace and World, Inc., 1962.

INDEX OF AUTHORS OF POETRY AND PROSE

INDEX OF TITLES OR FIRST LINES OF POETRY AND PROSE

ADDENDA